POUR OUT YOUR HEART

POUR OUT YOUR HEART

Discovering Joy, Strength, and Intimacy with God through Prayer

Jeremy Linneman

Copyright © 2025 by Jeremy Linneman
All Rights Reserved.
Printed in the United States of America

979-8-3845-0070-4

Published by B&H Publishing Group
Brentwood, Tennessee

Dewey Decimal Classification: 248.3
Subject Heading: GOD \ PRAYER \ SPIRITUAL LIFE

Unless otherwise noted, all Scripture references are taken from the New International Version®, NIV® Copyright ©1973, 1978, 1984, 2011 by Biblica, Inc.® Used by permission. All rights reserved worldwide.

Scripture references marked CSB are taken from the Christian Standard Bible. Copyright © 2017 by Holman Bible Publishers. Used by permission. Christian Standard Bible®, and CSB® are federally registered trademarks of Holman Bible Publishers, all rights reserved.

Scripture references marked MSG are taken from The Message, copyright © 1993, 2002, 2018 by Eugene H. Peterson.

Scripture references marked NLT are taken from the New Living Translation, copyright © 1996, 2004, 2015 by Tyndale House Foundation. Used by permission of Tyndale House Publishers, Inc., Carol Stream, Illinois 60188. All rights reserved.

Scripture references marked ESV are taken from the English Standard Version. ESV® Text Edition: 2016. Copyright © 2001 by Crossway Bibles, a publishing ministry of Good News Publishers.

Scripture references marked KJV are taken from The King James Version, public domain.

Cover design and illustration by Matt Lehman.
Author photo by Jessica Linneman.

1 2 3 4 5 6 • 28 27 26 25

A prayer for all those who are dry, disconnected, or stuck:

For those who haven't felt the warmth of God's presence—
For those who struggle to relate to God as Father—
For those who can't find joy or peace in this life—
For those who feel trapped in relationships of hurt, abuse, and emptiness—
For those ensnared in the grip of poverty, mistreatment, and addiction—
For the chronically sick and sore, the depressed, the anxious—
For the orphan, the stranger, and the widow—

Father God,
All-powerful God of heaven and earth, of mountaintop and wilderness,
Heal the sick; bind up the broken; restore the lonely.
Set the captives free, O God.
Fill us with your Holy Spirit.
Make us like your beloved Son.
Grant us your joy, peace, and strength now and forever.

Let the outpourings of our hearts be precious in your sight.
Through Christ our King,
Amen and amen.

Contents

Introduction	1
1. Receiving the Father's Embrace	9
2. What Do You Want?	33
3. Pour Out Your Hearts Like Water	55
4. Heart-at-Rest Prayer	75
5. Heaven-on-Earth Prayer	99
6. Praying through Heartache	119
7. Cultivating a Hunger for God	141
8. Prayer as Walking by the Spirit	161
9. In the End, Everything Turns to Praise	179
A Final Word	195
Acknowledgments	207
Notes	211

Introduction

A few weeks ago, my friend Todd pulled me aside after our community group gathering. We had finished our discussion time with about twenty minutes of prayer together, and he was both challenged and encouraged. He said, "I've been a Christian for decades, but I've never learned to pray." He continued, "I know I'm supposed to pray. But I don't know what to do. I love Bible study, and I like serving. But for some reason I can't explain, I just don't really pray."

I have some version of this conversation at least monthly, typically when a new person or couple joins our church and is trying to make sense of our significant emphasis on prayer. Why is this the case? Why is prayer so difficult? If prayer is such a constant theme in the Scriptures from beginning to end, why do many Christians feel like they don't know how to pray and feel little desire to develop a praying life?

Of course, there are many folks who love prayer. They don't just value prayer as a concept; they actually pray. Deeply. They believe it really does something. They feel intimately connected to God, and as a result, their lives are marked by a gentleness, increasing maturity, and relational quality that many of us are seeking. What do they know that we don't?

There are many reasons why prayer doesn't come easily for us. We're busy people. We haven't been trained in prayer. It's just difficult to sit still for more than five minutes without sweating in distraction. These are all true, but I think it goes deeper than all this. And recently, an unexpected source helped me see this clearly.

Ricky Gervais is a British comedian and actor best known for writing and starring in the original BBC version of *The Office*. Gervais's standup comedy specials are not exactly clean, and he is an outspoken atheist. But on a recent tour, he joked about his faith and shared his views on prayer.

> "People ask me, 'Do you pray?' No. I don't mind if you pray. People say 'I'm praying for you,' and I say 'thank you.' But if you cancel the chemotherapy, I'll say, 'Don't do that.' Do both. Pray and do the chemotherapy. Because doing both is the same as just doing the chemo. If you're going to do one, do the one that works."[1]

I laughed at first. Gervais is a master of delivery. But then something settled in like a dark cloud. At the time, I had been a Christian for most of my life—one who regularly prayed at the start of every day. But as I reflected, I realized Gervais's remarks might indeed represent my own view of prayer more than the biblical vision. More than *might*; they did. My commitment to prayer was often agnostic—as if I believed in the existence of the Divine and mentally assented to the importance of prayer, but didn't engage deeply with a personal, living God.

If you witnessed the weakness and inconsistency of my prayers in that season of my life, you'd likely conclude that I didn't really expect all that much out of prayer, opting instead for the things that "worked."

Following my life closely, you'd undoubtedly conclude that I relied far more on my intellect than the Holy Spirit, more on my own energies than the power of God. You'd watch every morning pass as I, functionally speaking, said a few weak prayers and then opened my eyes, laced up my Nikes, and got to work as if it all depended on me.

Or at least, that's until a few years ago, when I began to discover the joy and power of prayer.

Toward the end of 2019, I was experiencing a dangerous level of fatigue and apathy. Nothing was utterly falling apart—I've been there before, and this wasn't that—but I was struggling through daily life. My spiritual life was dry, and I could barely feel God's presence and love. Our little church plant was stumbling through its infancy stage, and our three boys were wonderful and exhausting at once. I was keeping my rhythms of Scripture, prayer, and fellowship, but I felt discouraged and powerless.

I was running on the mercies and energy of the past, and I was reaching the bottom of the tank. I began crying out to God with a mixture of lament, accusation, and petition. Desperation, as it turns out, is a key ingredient in prayer.

In this wilderness season, I cried out to God in the spirit of Lamentations 2:19:

> Arise, cry out in the night,
>   as the watches of the night begin;
> *pour out your heart like water*
>   in the presence of the Lord. (emphasis added)

The Lord met me powerfully and gently in that wilderness season of pouring out my heart. I can't say it was a sudden or explosive experience—like the ones I've read about in memoirs by Augustine and Blaise Pascal—and I didn't reach the third heaven. But nonetheless, over the course of a few days, I felt swept up in the powerful mercies of God. His presence felt so real and tangible. His Word leaped off the page. I prayed for hours on end. I even gave fasting another try after years of avoiding it.

Now, let's be clear: I have not become a prayer expert, nor have I become a super Christian. My journey is simply deepening. Said another way, I've come to understand these moments as personal "times of refreshing . . . from the Lord" (Acts 3:19). For the next few months, my prayer life came fully alive. I had newfound energy for life. My sweet wife, Jessie, was overjoyed I had been lifted from my funk. My boys could notice a difference in me. In my ministry relationships, I timidly brought up my renewal to our leaders, and several of them were experiencing something similar. Something remarkable was happening.

Over the past few years, my prayer life has ebbed and flowed; many dry seasons and powerless morning quiet times have come and gone. But as I've pressed further into the presence of God, he has been gracious and faithful to meet me with an increased love for him and for others. Perhaps you know this feeling well too. Or perhaps you long for it.

These days, I'm simply asking for *more*—more of God's presence, more of his Spirit's fruit ripening in my life, more Christlikeness as I walk with Jesus. To seek more of God is not to be discontent, but rather it's a content, sitting-on-the-Father's-lap prayer of a weaned child, seeking to be fully engaged in God's presence (Ps. 131:2).

These days, I still reflect on the comedian's words—"don't do prayer, *do something that works.*" But I'm also seeking to remind myself just how much prayer really does.

What Exactly Does Prayer Do?

Prayer welcomes us into the embrace of the Father and retrains us to live from belovedness.

Prayer uncovers our fragmented lives and invites us into wholehearted living.

Prayer is the means by which God moves history toward the renewal of all things; it leads to breakthrough.

Prayer invites us to face pain and suffering with honesty and hope.

Prayer opens us to a life of celebration and thanksgiving and teaches us to praise.

Prayer connects us to other believers more deeply and the mission of God more fruitfully.

Prayer increases our experience of the Holy Spirit's presence and power.

Prayer reorients us to eternity—the coming new creation.

In short, prayer does stuff. And I'm not the only one who has discovered this.

Over the past few years, along with my own spiritual awakening, our little church has caught a vision for prayer. We have a long way to go, but we have become a praying church. Our calendar is filled with prayer meetings, and people are praying with joy, passion, and power. We've seen people experience profound inner healing. We've seen marriages restored. Members have seen their long-time friends come to Christ and be baptized. Lives are being changed, and it's not our music, our level of production, and (certainly not) our preaching. It's prayer.

Our lives are powerless apart from prayer. Prayer is the way in which we enter the presence of God and gain access to his strength, peace, and wisdom. And the more we experience God's presence in prayer, the more we will keep turning to him. Prayer cultivates a hunger for God. Prayer makes us more content (we are happy with *less*) and hungrier for God's presence (we only want *more*). But that doesn't mean it comes easily.

I wonder if you can relate. Do you struggle with busyness, distraction, and, most deeply, the plaguing fear that prayer might not do much at all? And do you know why you have this plaguing fear? Because you've been lied to your entire life, just as I have. You've been told that everything depends on you. As a result, you move through life in a lonely, anxious hurry. You must grind. You must hustle. You must *make things happen*.

But life is not supposed to be a grand flurry of effort.

When you approach our Father with the posture of an eager child, with a humble faith and spirit of expectation, you really can receive a heart at rest and move out into the world with joy, peace, and power. If you're holding this book, I believe it's because you hear a gentle voice within calling you deeper. You want to pray with joy and power. You want your life to go ==deeper in lament and higher in praise.== You want more of God. You want *something*.

Why hold it all in? He knows what you want and need. Pour it out. And God promises to pour his own joy, peace, and strength into you. "Pour out your hearts to him, for God is our refuge" (Ps. 62:8). "Give all your worries and cares to God, for he cares about you" (1 Pet. 5:7 NLT). "Pile your troubles on GOD's shoulders—he'll carry your load, he'll help you out" (Ps. 55:22 MSG).

He really means it. Come before the living God and pour out your heart. Don't worry about getting your prayers right. Don't try to clean up your thoughts and feelings first. Don't hold back; he can handle it. Pour out your fears, frustrations, and struggles; pour out your hopes and dreams and desires. Let it flow like water.

Pour out your heart, and God will pour something back into your heart. He will fill it with joy, peace, and strength. He will pour his very own love and power into your life. This is the invitation to prayer.

If this is what you want to experience—if you're ready for a ==deeper, more vibrant, more unpredictable life with God==—then keep reading.

Father,
You are our hearts' truest desire.
Thank you for calling us to yourself.
Thank you for the Son, opening the way back home for us.
Thank you for the Spirit, revealing who you are and empowering our lives.
Thank you for leaping off the porch to embrace us when we turn back to you.
Oh Lord, we need more of you. Or at least, we want to want more of you.
Come, Lord. Amen and amen.

1

Receiving the Father's Embrace

I grew up in a wildly charismatic church in the 1980s. And I mean *really charismatic*—think open mic for prophecy, regular testimonies of miraculous healing, and plenty of flags and banners. (So many banners!)

On one hand, it was wonderful. There was true delight in worship, there was complete embrace of risk and faith, and there was a sense of expectation in prayer. On the other hand, there were many excesses, and emphasis was often misplaced. The preaching of the gospel was not consistent and balanced. And unfortunately, there were some deeply hurtful abuses of position and power.

As I look back on the years spent within that community of faith, one thing always sticks out in my memory: the simple, self-forgetful, childlike faith.

In my adult years, I came to discover and embrace Reformed theology, expository preaching, and the beauty of the liturgical and contemplative traditions. I am deeply thankful for my current body of faith here. But I haven't lost that early experience of happy delight in the presence and people of God.

These days, I'm hopeful that in my lifetime, I will see the best of these two traditions come together more fully. In the meantime, I'll admit a secondary aim of this book: to help my beloved Reformed brothers and sisters learn from the passion, simplicity, and power of their charismatic counterparts. (Much more on this later.)

Perhaps no one has expressed the need for this synergy more than the modern-day Reformed patriarch, Ray Ortlund Jr. In a podcast for The Gospel Coalition, Ortlund reflected on growing up in the Jesus Movement of the sixties and later joining the Reformed, gospel-centered tradition. He said:

> I don't think that we generally—we gospel [centered] types—we have not experienced a corresponding resurgence of relational beauty. . . . We've all been so enriched and strengthened and helped, and the truth of the gospel has been clarified for us all. But we have not had the same resurgence of relational beauty. I don't know anybody that's downright mean. But . . . we need to—very carefully, reverently, joyously—attend to, cultivate, and build the intangibles of the relational beauties that the gospel itself calls for and creates.[1]

In other words, you can believe in the *gospel*, hold to solid theology, and enjoy well-ordered churches and yet barely experience the *relational beauty of Christ*. What a tragic loss! Who told us we have to choose between the truth of God and the presence of God? I'm not interested in a faith that considers God's Word and intimacy with him to be an "either/or." No one would say this explicitly, but our churches often represent one to the exclusion of the other.

In my own life, in my pastoral ministry, and—to be clear, in this book—I am eagerly rejecting this "either-or." I'm pursuing the "both-and." I'm setting out to embrace two things: ==the clear, once-for-all *gospel truth* and its result, a burning passion for the *relational presence* of God. Gospel and presence. Word and Spirit. Doctrine and delight.==

How do we cultivate a life like this? How do we hold these things together? I believe the answer lies in Jesus's most well-known teaching on prayer.

Jesus must have been delighted when his disciples asked him how to pray. I mean, his disciples asked Jesus *a lot* of bad questions.

When the Samaritans don't welcome Jesus in their town, James and John ask, "Lord, do you want us to call fire down from heaven to destroy them?" (Luke 9:54). Not surprisingly, Jesus rebukes them. At the moment of Jesus's transfiguration, Peter says, "I will put up three shelters—one for you, one for Moses and one for Elijah" (Matt. 17:4). Mark and Luke's Gospels makes sure we know, for all time, Peter did *not* know what he was talking about (Mark 9:6; Luke 9:33).

But occasionally they get it right. "Teach us to pray," they ask (Luke 11:1). Our Lord must have been beaming with joy at the opportunity to teach his beloved friends how to enjoy fellowship with his Father. For this question, he doesn't rebuke them. He doesn't ignore them. He teaches them.

How Not to Pray: The Pharisee's Prayer

Interestingly, Jesus doesn't begin his teaching with how to pray but how *not* to pray. He points them toward the religious leaders of the day. "When you pray, do not be like the hypocrites, for they love to pray standing in the synagogues and on the street corners to be seen by others" (Matt. 6:5). In other words, as the most important theology book of our generation (Sally Lloyd-Jones's *Jesus Storybook Bible*) puts it, "They really weren't praying as much as just showing off. They used lots of special words that were so clever, no one understood what they meant."²

Jesus sets before us one way to pray, a posture we might take: It's the Pharisee's prayer. The Pharisee (or hypocrite) prays, in the words of Jesus himself, *to be seen by others*. In a world obsessed with image, appearance, and perfection, even prayer can become a means of gaining others' attention and approval. We'll look at this in more detail in the next chapter, but it's important to see the contrast before Jesus invites us into the correct posture.

But When You Pray: The Child's Prayer

The first approach to prayer that Jesus describes is the hypocrite's prayer—the overflow of a performative spirituality, rooted in insecurity. What, then, is the proper approach to prayer? Jesus next describes how to rightly approach God. "But when you pray, go into your room, close the door and pray to your Father, who is unseen. Then your Father, who sees what is done in secret, will reward you" (Matt. 6:6).

Where the hypocrite plans his prayers and takes them out to the synagogues and street corners, Jesus's disciples are to stay at home, go into their rooms (in the Greek, the word typically referred to a pantry or closet) and close the door. The hypocrite prays to be seen by others; the disciple prays to be seen by God.

But this posture is not merely the disciple's prayer; Jesus goes one step further. Remember, he says, "pray to *your Father*, who is unseen" (6:6, emphasis added).

Now, let's pause and let the full weight of this phrase sink in. The Israelites had thousands of years of history following God. They had the stories of creation and the garden, they knew the lives of Abraham, Isaac, and Jacob; they had the wisdom of the Proverbs and had memorized many Psalms. They worshipped in the temple, gave tithes to the poor and needy, observed the Sabbath, and celebrated dozens of holy days. Their lives were appropriately religious and (in varying degrees depending on the person) God-centered.

But this was new. Although the Old Testament occasionally refers to God as Father to his people (Deut. 32:6; Ps. 103:13; Isa. 63:16; 64:8), this was not a regular thought for the people of God. For Israel, God is predominately known as Creator, Redeemer, Shepherd, and Almighty God. But Father? Let's not get too carried away.

But suddenly, Jesus is on the scene; he's the Son of God and the exact imprint of God; he is "one with the Father" (John 10:30). He is, to quote the *Jesus Storybook Bible* again, "everything God wanted to say to the world, in a person."³

Sure, God loves to be Jesus's Father, we might think. After all, Jesus is doing a pretty good job of being a Son. He is eternal and perfect and holy. He doesn't sin. He never disappoints his Father. Why wouldn't God *love* his Son, Jesus? We believe all this. But God as *our* Father? Here we may stumble. Yet Jesus was abundantly clear.

> "Close the door and pray to *your* Father." (Matt. 6:6, emphasis added)

"Then *your* Father . . . will reward *you*." (v. 6, emphasis added)

"Do not be like [the pagans], for *your* Father knows what *you* need." (v. 8, emphasis added)

"This, then, is how *you* should pray: '*Our* Father in heaven.'" (v. 9, emphasis added)

"If you forgive other people when they sin against you, *your* heavenly Father will also forgive *you*." (v. 14, emphasis added)

"But if you do not forgive others their sins, *your* Father will not forgive *your* sins." (v. 15, emphasis added)

There we go: Six references to God as Father—and not just Father to Jesus, but Father to *you*—in Jesus's very brief instructions on how to pray. Do you see the posture Jesus invites us to take? It is simply and boldly *the child's prayer*.

Rediscovering God as Father

What's the difference between approaching God as merely a strong and powerful and compassionate God and approaching him first and foremost as our Father? This difference will be felt throughout all of life, but nowhere more deeply than in prayer.

Many people struggle to approach God as Father and understandably so. Many folks that I sit with have only known "father" to be a hurtful person or complicated relationship.

Adoption is one of the most important and beautiful elements of the gospel, some would even say the core message of Christianity.

It reveals God's heart and unlocks the Scriptures for us in a way nothing else does. Spiritual adoption is simply the truth that God makes us his own sons and daughters when he saves us through the work of his Son Jesus. He didn't have to make us sons and daughters. It would have been enough to make us part of his kingdom, as citizens or servants. But we learn of God's heart when we witness something unexpected: he doesn't stop there.

Though it's a wonder that God would make us citizens of his kingdom, the truth is he doesn't need slaves or servants or citizens. He doesn't need anything. But he wants something. *He wants children.* The theologian J. I. Packer has said if you want to know how well a person understands Christianity, "find out how much he makes of the thought of being God's child, and having God as his Father. If this is not the thought that prompts and controls his worship and prayers and his whole outlook on life, it means that he does not understand Christianity very well at all."[4]

Some years ago, my sister and her husband went through the long and difficult and expensive process of adoption. Anthony was born into a difficult environment in a different part of town. My sister and her husband had been wanting to adopt for years, they worked with an agency, they did home studies, they saved money, they filled out paperwork, and finally they became Anthony's foster parents. After years as Anthony's foster parents, the process was completed, and they went to the courthouse together. Finally, the judge declared Anthony to belong to Drew and Sarah and banged his gavel. At long last, he legally belonged to them. It's objective, it's definitive, it's legally-binding, it's forever. And yet, it was far more than a legal transaction. It represented something so beautiful. Though there is certainly loss and complication involved, a child in need now has a safe, new home.

That's the good news of adoption. You were an orphan, homeless and hopeless in a dangerous world. But God put in the work, took the steps to do it legally, and then bent down and picked you up into his arms. As the apostle Paul put it, "those who are led by the Spirit of God are the children of God. The Spirit you received does not make you slaves, so that you live in fear again; rather, the Spirit you received brought about your adoption to sonship. And by him we cry, '*Abba,* Father'" (Rom. 8:14–15).

There's the exodus language: you are no longer slaves. But it's not just *salvation from*, it's also *salvation for*. We are saved *from* our old, broken ways of life, and we are saved *for* a vibrant life with God, as children in his royal family. Further, we're given the Holy Spirit, who brings about our adoption and testifies it's official. We can now cry out this phrase: "Abba Father."

God loves you—he's won you back, he's brought you in, he's crowned you with every bit of his inheritance, and he's filled you with his own Holy Spirit (Rom. 8:14–17). Oh, and this Spirit—God himself dwelling in our hearts—is even still just a preview of something even better. The Spirit, Paul says, is an advance payment of the perfect communion we'll have in the new heavens and earth for all eternity (Eph. 1:13–14).

How on earth do we respond to all this? We should be overwhelmed with gratitude, praise, relief, and joy. We should live a new kind of life—the life not of an orphan or slave, but of a beloved child. We should look in the mirror every morning and recall the unimaginable: *God didn't need me. He wanted me. And he moved heaven and earth for me to be his child.*

A Life of Belovedness

Galatians 4:6 says, "Because you are his sons, God sent the Spirit of his Son into our hearts, the Spirit who calls out, '*Abba*, Father.'" Isn't it interesting that both Galatians 4 and Romans 8 use the phrase, "*Abba* Father," when talking about adoption?

Abba is an Aramaic word for "father." For Jesus, it meant acceptance, relationship, and intimacy. *Abba* was so important to Jesus that his followers left it untranslated in their gospel narratives. There's no other word quite like it.

Do you remember the most famous use of *Abba* coming from the heart of Jesus? It was in the garden of Gethsemane. On the night of his betrayal, just before his death, he led his disciples to this garden around midnight. He prayed and prayed, while his friends kept falling asleep.

Side note: How utterly *human* is it that at Jesus's most vulnerable, painful moment, he just wanted his friends by his side? And—another side note—Jesus desperately wanted his friends to enter with him into his pain, but they weren't ready. How often do we just want our spouse or friends or mentors to enter fully into our pain, yet they can't? Surely some things are for us to carry alone into the garden, to learn to depend on the Father alone.

So Jesus is on his knees, alone, middle of the night, weeping, sweating blood. He prays, "*Abba* Father." Rarely, or perhaps never, would any Hebrew teacher or theologian use *Abba* to speak to God. This, after all, was a simple word used by small children before advanced words were learned.

"*Abba*." It is our first word in life, before our minds and bodies are fully developed. "*Abba*." It may be our last word in life—as our bodies and minds fail us at last. Indeed, God is our Alpha and Omega, our beginning and end, but at both points and between, he is still our *Abba*.

The Love of God Makes Us Radically Secure

When you know love of the Father on an *Abba* level, you are radically secure. You have probably met Christians like this. They live with a childlike faith and spirituality. Their natural posture looks like this:

Childlike Spirituality

Posture	God is my Father, I am his beloved child.
Default mode	I love God and am freely loved by him.
God's view of me	God delights in me and sings over me. I trust that the eyes of the Lord are on his children.
Toward others	I focus on loving and serving others. I seek to show grace and restore others in a spirit of gentleness. I am open, teachable, grateful for growth opportunities, resilient.
Present to others	I am close, secure, capable of relational intimacy.
Finds comfort	I am safe in the Father's presence and love.
Toward time	I am rarely in a hurry; I work from rest.
In the church	I am content to be with Jesus and serve where needed; I see my brothers and sisters as family, not as threats or as burdens.
Prayer	I find prayer a joy and source of continual strength.
Suffering	I see hardship as an opportunity to learn to trust the Father more deeply.

As you look at this list, what are you drawn to? Do you believe this type of life is possible? Perhaps you knew this life once but have lost it since. Whatever the case, you likely want this kind of life to be possible. If you're reading this book, you almost certainly long for a life of joy, strength, and intimacy with God.

So how do we get it? The only way to a life of childlike spirituality is to first get the love of God deep in our hearts.

There are a few types of videos that really get me, but none more than candid moments where a child discovers she's been adopted. Picture it: a foster child is sitting with her foster parents, and they give her a gift to open. She opens it up; it's framed paperwork. "What does it say?" she asks. It's an adoption certificate. "It says you belong to us now." The girl bursts into tears. She reaches for them, and they embrace her, and neither will let each other go.

This, my friends, is how we need to picture Christianity. It's not about following the rules. It's not about fitting into a group of people. It's not solely about justification by faith, or even repentance and conversion. After all, what are we saved *into* anyway? The family of God! Everything else flows downstream from being adopted by a gracious and compassionate Father.

The challenge, then, is believing this. The apostle Paul prayed that we might have all the spiritual strength of God—all the almighty, universe-creating, soul-redeeming, eternal power of God—for this one thing, to know the love of Christ (Eph. 3:14–21). It takes a mighty work of God to get his love deep within us. The greatest challenge in the Christian life is getting the love of the Father into our hearts. We might mentally assent to God's love. We might know all the verses and creeds affirming it. But are we really living in his love? Has the love of God become the air we breathe and the water we drink?

As Paul wrote in Romans 5:5, "God's love has been poured out into our hearts through the Holy Spirit, who has been given to us."

What a life-changing verse! The Father wants to *pour* his love into your heart through the Holy Spirit. Yet so many of us have not entered into the deep, abiding security of the love of God.

Insecure Spirituality

There's an epidemic in our churches, and it seems to be true across evangelical, charismatic, mainline Protestant, and Catholic churches. Like most epidemics, it's invisible but widespread. It's an epidemic of insecurity. We believers are remarkably insecure. Before you take that as an insult, let me explain. It might just be the key to discovering a freshness, depth, and secure love you've never known before.

Insecurity is a state of life where we are not safe and sheltered in someone or something's strength and affection. Many places are quite unsafe: prison, an open body of water, middle school. And Christianity can also be a deeply insecure place; that is, if we haven't fully grasped the good news of our union with Christ and adoption.

This is the good news of Christianity: when we put our faith in Jesus, turning from our sins and following him, we are joined to him as one. The Father accepts the Son's death in our place—the payment for a penalty that our sin has created. We are restored to the Father; he forgives our sins and receives us into his vast and unending love. Like the father in the parable of the prodigal son, he welcomes us gladly and calls for a celebration. We become united to Jesus; so what's true of him is now true of us—we are accepted, we are children of God, we are heirs of his eternal kingdom. And what belongs to Jesus now belongs to us—we have right standing before God and we have inexhaustible spiritual riches. And further, as a seal and guarantee of all this (and our final, future salvation), we receive the Holy Spirit, who is generously poured out into our hearts to indwell us with power and Christlike character. One day, Christ will return, the dead will be raised, we will be given perfect, resurrection bodies, all sin, brokenness, and death will be destroyed forever; and we will enjoy life with God for all eternity in a heavenly new creation.

Good news, right? So why then do so many of us struggle to grasp this remarkable life with God? Why do so many Christians believe in Jesus, get their salvation secured, and then go on living a generally unchanged life? Why are so many of us still so timid toward God and others? I believe it has to do with a limited understanding of God's love for us, a failure to fully grasp the beauty, power, and security that comes with being a beloved child of God.

Richard Lovelace, a church historian and theologian I have spent the past decade reading and re-reading, put it like this:

> Christians who are no longer sure that God loves and accepts them in Jesus, apart from their present spiritual achievements, are subconsciously radically insecure persons—much less secure than non-Christians, because they have too much light to rest easily under the constant bulletins they receive from their Christian environment about the holiness of God and the righteousness they are supposed to have.[5]

Consider what Lovelace is saying. If we believe our standing before God depends on our spiritual achievements (that is, our obedience, our recent Bible reading, our service to the church, tithing, and so on), then we will be radically insecure. In fact, we will be more insecure than even non-Christians, whose conscience doesn't continually convict them of sin and who aren't regularly reminded of their need of the gospel.

If this is true (and I believe it is), just think of the way it will shape our lives. A spirituality uncertain of God's love will always have to perform. It will always have to prove. It will always have to defend. It will always be scheming and striving, and it will never be at rest. An insecure spirituality is a brutal type of life.

Insecure Spirituality Is Always Performing

In our church, we use the phrase "performative spirituality" to describe the default position of our hearts toward God and prayer. (I'm not exactly sure where this phrase originates, but I've heard it from New York City pastors Jon Tyson and John Starke. The charts you'll find below were actually inspired by something Jon Tyson presented in a sermon, and some of the language within the charts comes from him.[6]) Most simply, performative spirituality is performance-based religion. It's living to get God's approval and affection. It's an act to convince yourself you're becoming a better Christian and more useful to God and others.

Let me be clear: performative spirituality comes straight from the pit of hell. Nothing robs us of more joy. Nothing is more assured to give us either religious pride (if we're performing well) or spiritual despair (if we're performing poorly). Nothing is better at producing superficial, impersonal, and powerless prayers.

Why? Because the performance-based approach to Christianity puts us on a stage to earn God's acceptance and approval. That's the extent of our relationship with him. That's the best we get with this spiritual posture. It's an exhausting posture, and Scripture says nothing good of it. The biblical approach is this: we're not on a stage, we're in a *relationship*. We're not performers, we're *children*. And God is not a harsh director or dissatisfied critic, he is our *Father*.

Have you been living by the wrong posture? Have you been prevented from receiving the embrace of the Father because you're too busy trying to impress him and others? Have you been held back from a deeper life with God by your own incessant need to strive, hide, and try every possible path of self-improvement?

And what about your church? Have your church members been hustling themselves to death instead of seeking to become deeply formed, wonderfully fruitful disciples of Jesus? Do you look around and see a preoccupation with superficial "three keys to a happy life" teaching, excellence in production (ahem, performance), and an avoidance of the deep and difficult aspects of Christian living—all for the sake of comfort and church growth?

What is the result of this? Millions of believers who read their Bibles, sort of pray, and go to church with decent regularity—and yet are simultaneously dry spiritually and unchanged in their Christlikeness. They may read of God's power and love every day. They may hear the gospel week after week. But none of it seems to make a practical difference. They are still insecure, day after day. Despite all they know and do, their natural posture in life looks like this:

Insecure Spirituality

Posture	God is my boss, I am his servant; God is the critic, I am the performer.
Default mode	I'm on my own; nothing good happens unless I make it happen.
God's view of me	God wants me to do better; he's a bit disappointed, or he is distant and busy; he's not actively engaged in my life, or God is fine with things as long as I perform decently enough.
Toward others	I live to be seen by others, craving their approval.
	I greatly fear being exposed as a fraud.
	I tend to be critical, comparative, competitive, easily angered, easily hurt.
	I often see others as a threat or a burden.
Present to others	I am conditional and distant.
	I am always comparing—constantly aware of where I (and others) rank.
Finds comfort	I find comfort in busyness, addiction, distraction, and empty religious activity—whatever makes me look good or feel appreciated.
Toward time	I am typically in a hurry; I struggle to slow down and rest.
In the church	I seek positions of honor, power, and influence.
Prayer	My prayers are sporadic, scattered, and distracted.
	I often feel guilty: "I should pray more."
Suffering	I am non-resilient, unable to handle challenges and trials of life without bitterness.
	I view suffering as a sign that God is not with me or against me.

Unfortunately, this chart wasn't difficult for me to create. I am so familiar with the orphan's heart that it's still so regularly my default mode. I've been grinding all my life. I've been working and scheming and defending and protecting and projecting. Why? Because I assume everything depends on me. Even when I say otherwise, my actions and stress level suggest it. And from my years of pastoring, I know that I'm not alone in this struggle.

Further, I'm afraid many times we see this insecurity within us and yet continue to choose it. It's safer. It's worked for us so far. We subconsciously say, "Because of my insecure heart, I've got this great degree, this job, status in the world. I don't want to lose all that." What would happen if we actually set this insecure, performing lifestyle aside? I mean, the reason we hold on is because it *works* in a world teeming with other performance addicts. If we give up the praise and approval of others, will we survive?

Thankfully, Scripture gives us an answer. There's a case study in insecure, performative spirituality in the New Testament, and it's the Pharisees.[7] As Jesus says, everything they did was for others' praise: They loved to take the seats of honor, to be recognized and praised in public, and to be identified according to their social status (Matt. 23:5–7). They were outwardly impressive but inwardly corrupt (vv. 25–27). They drew near to wealth and despised the poor and needy (Luke 11:39–44). Even those who believed in Jesus did so privately, because they loved the praise of the crowds more than the approval of God (John 12:42–43). In short, they were hypocrites; they were play actors, putting a mask on and playing a part (Luke 12:1).

The Pharisees were a comparing, scheming, joyless bunch of religious leaders. But beneath it all, they were radically insecure. And their insecurity manifested in, as it always does, a low (and even murderous) view of others and an unwillingness to accept those outside their tribe. Now, if we're honest, we should admit that this ancient religious group is essentially a natural extension of something that exists in each of us too. Living without God's fatherly love makes anyone—you, me, or a Pharisee—radically insecure, and from this insecurity, we feel the need to perform, prove ourselves, and defend ourselves. That's what they were doing. That's what all of us are doing apart from the safety and shelter of our Father's strength and affection.

As my mentor-friend Scotty Smith likes to say, "You can hear the lyric of the gospel and still not feel the music." This is what performative spirituality does best; it robs our lives of its rhythm and dance. But if we can identify and uproot this performance-based mentality, we can open ourselves to a deep, personal, and powerful life of prayer.

So the question is, do you want to live your whole life like a Pharisee? Or like a child? Consider the trajectory of your life and faith. How do you want to end up? Angry, moody, and murderous in heart? Always on the defense and proving yourself? Or would you rather operate out of a heart that is safe, stable, and open to the world? Able to laugh at misunderstandings instead of getting offended by them? Not having to prove yourself in every room? Free and secure.

Jesus offers you the choice.

Truth be told, there will always be people who resist the Father's loving embrace, and so the performance epidemic will likely exist in some degree till Christ returns. But for those of us who want out of that spiraling vortex of shame and death, we can do something about it now. If I remember anything from my infectious disease studies in college, in an epidemic, we must notice common symptoms, identify the cause, and find a cure for the infection.

Lucky for us, we're two-thirds of the way through. We've already listed the common symptoms above (Insecure Spirituality list), and we've already identified the cause (Performance-Based living). What's left is to embrace the cure: putting off the orphan's heart and regaining our child's heart—one trained in receiving the love of our Father. Said another way, the cure is to release insecure spirituality and replace it with something much better. After all, the orphan's heart will never be satisfied. It's looking for its Father all along. Nothing else will do. Getting the love of the Father deep into our hearts is the only way.

Releasing and Replacing Insecure Spirituality

At this point, we might see the presence of insecure spirituality in our hearts and turn to guilt and obedience. "Don't be insecure!" we tell ourselves. Sadly, many sermons and counseling sessions can do the same: "Stop worrying!" The subtle message we can turn to is just another version of performance-based religion—"Just try harder." But this is not a work of willpower; it's a gift of the Holy Spirit, one that we participate in by God's grace, releasing and replacing insecurity spirituality.

To help us do this in a practical way, let's compare the two charts we've seen so far. Side by side, we can see what insecure, performative spirituality looks like next to a childlike, secure spirituality that flows from the Father's love.

Childlike Spirituality

Posture	God is my Father, I am his beloved child.
Default mode	I love God and am freely loved by him.
God's view of me	God delights in me and sings over me.
	I trust that the eyes of the Lord are on his children.
Toward others	I focus on loving and serving others.
	I seek to show grace and restore others in a spirit of gentleness.
	I am open, teachable, grateful for growth opportunities, resilient.
Present to others	I am close, secure, capable of relational intimacy.
Finds comfort	I am safe in the Father's presence and love.
Toward time	I am rarely in a hurry; I work from rest.
In the church	I am content to be with Jesus and serve where needed; I see my brothers and sisters as family, not as threats or as burdens.
Prayer	I find prayer a joy and source of continual strength.
Suffering	I see hardship as an opportunity to learn to trust the Father more deeply.

(margin note: Zeph 3:17)

Insecure Spirituality

Posture	God is my boss, I am his servant; God is the critic, I am the performer.
Default mode	I'm on my own; nothing good happens unless I make it happen.
God's view of me	God wants me to do better; he's a bit disappointed, or He is distant and busy; he's not actively engaged in my life, or God is fine with things as long as I perform decently enough.
Toward others	I live to be seen by others, craving their approval.
	I greatly fear being exposed as a fraud.
	I tend to be critical, comparative, competitive, easily angered, easily hurt.
	I often see others as a threat or a burden.
Present to others	I am conditional and distant.
	I am always comparing—constantly aware of where I (and others) rank.
Finds comfort	I find comfort in busyness, addiction, distraction, and empty religious activity—whatever makes me look good or feel appreciated.
Toward time	I am typically in a hurry; I struggle to slow down and rest.
In the church	I seek positions of honor, power, and influence.
Prayer	My prayers are sporadic, scattered, and distracted.
	I often feel guilty: "I should pray more."
Suffering	I am non-resilient, unable to handle challenges and trials of life without bitterness.
	I view suffering as a sign that God is not with me or against me.

Looking at these charts, which one better represents you? Or better yet, where do you see yourself moving back and forth? If you're like me, you see a lot of uncomfortable evidence that an insecure, performative way of life has taken some root in you. So what are we to do?

We can release and replace. Release insecurity, and replace it with the Father's love. While it sounds too simple to be true, it is a pattern that will be fruitful over and over again as we walk in the childlike faith that Jesus commends.

In other words, another kind of life is available to us. Once we have identified the source of our insecurity, and traced how it shows up in a performance-based lifestyle, we'll be able to pull it up from the roots. This lie from the pit of hell can be dragged out into the light and left to suffocate and die in the light of God's love. And instead, a different type of life can take root in the good soil of Jesus's life. And once we've identified, broken, and released this insecure, performative spirituality, a confident new life of prayer can be opened to us.

Imagine you walk into the next member's meeting at your church—no, wait, let's say it's a well-attended prayer gathering. You step into a lobby full of people, and immediately you notice three of your friends chatting together. They just happen to be popular, "in crowd" leaders in the church. You wonder if it's safe to approach them, but suddenly wonder, *Am I good enough to join this group? Am I on their level? What if they turn away from me? Worse—what if they're talking about me already?!* As soon as you recognize that anxious, performance-minded, self-focused narrative start running in your mind, silently pray. Release it to the Father. Ask for his help. Now imagine you look across the room and see a person standing alone. You haven't met them before, and it seems like they might not know anyone in the gathering. You have now released your anxious, performing feelings and are free to replace them with God's peace and a focus on others. You walk up and introduce yourself, make small talk, and then invite your new friend to come meet your three other friends. Congratulations: you've taken one more baby step in releasing anxious spirituality and replacing it with the love of the Father—for you and others.

Praying from Belovedness

When Jesus taught his disciples how to pray, remember, he began by teaching them how *not* to pray. Don't pray like the Pharisees; pray instead like little children. Don't pray from insecurity; pray from belovedness. Don't pray to get God's approval and affection; pray *from* God's approval and affection. Jesus is setting two postures before us. Our prayer lives depend on which posture we take, moment by moment, day after day.

The Scriptures often set before us two paths to evaluate side-by-side. We can build our house on the sand or on a solid foundation; we can take the broad path or the narrow one; we can remain in the darkness or live in the light. Moses's famous words in Deuteronomy 30—though they are primarily about following God's Word—form an appropriate secondary challenge to each of us as we compare insecure, performative spirituality with a secure, childlike spiritual life.

> This day I call the heavens and the earth as witnesses against you that I have set before you life and death, blessings and curses. Now *choose life*, so that you and your children may live and that you may love the LORD your God, listen to his voice,

and hold fast to him. (Deut. 30:19–20, emphasis added)

Jesus is doing nothing less than inviting us into the Father's embrace. He's challenging us to lay down our pride, self-sufficiency, and performative life. And he's inviting us to approach God as Father—a good and loving, ever-present, all-knowing and all-powerful Father. He has set before us a way of life and death. And he's compelling us, "Choose life!" See the destructive patterns of performative spirituality. See how weary and dry it makes you! See how the embrace of the Father gives you the deep security you've always wanted.

Again, Jesus offers you the choice.

Remembering the Truth (and Praying It)

This is where we must begin our praying lives: God is our good and loving Father. He has done all the work to prepare our adoption. Jesus is our atoning sacrifice (1 John 2:2). He was forsaken on the cross (Matt. 27:46) that we might be adopted. And now, he's also our big brother, intercessor, and advocate (Rom. 8:17, 29; Heb. 7:25; 1 John 2:1). The Holy Spirit is God's abiding presence within us and our promise of future good (1 Cor. 3:16; Eph. 1:14). He brings about our adoption (Rom. 8:15–17). The Spirit takes our orphan's heart, aching to be welcomed in, and transforms it into the heart of a beloved child.

So now God is, in essence, saying to you: "I have all that I need. I don't need any slaves; I don't need servants; I don't need good, law-abiding citizens. What I *want* first and foremost is children."

Say it again: God is my Father. I am a child of God. His love is better than life.

Pray it now: God, you are my Father. Because of your Son's work, I am *already* your beloved child—I do not have to perform to become one. Your love is better than life. In you, I have everything I need.

Abba Father,
We thank you and praise you
that you have called us sons and daughters.
Bring us now, Abba Father, into this beautiful reality more fully.
I lay my insecure spirituality before you.
I lay my performative mindset before you.
Turn my orphan's heart into a beloved child's heart.
Deepen your love in me;
let it be the air I breathe.
In Christ's name and power, amen and amen.

2

What Do You Want?

I don't watch much TV these days, so I rarely see any commercials anymore. But even I noticed that commercials in mid-2020 took on a totally new tone. This was, of course, in the midst of the Covid pandemic, and large corporations were scrambling to maintain their sales during a national lockdown. Let me remind you of the basic commercial script during these months.

Let's say the product is Reese's peanut butter cups. The scene opens with dramatic, inspiring music. There's a sunrise, or sunset, we're not sure. Children are dancing. They're talking with Grandma by video. Parents are smiling from their laptops. And the narrator, in a deep and reassuring voice, says: "In these uncertain times . . . now more than ever . . . we are resilient, we will make it through . . . nothing can stop us . . . Reese's. You can eat them at home."

Whatever the product, the message was the same. But immediately, an internal inconsistency was evident. "Nothing can stop us," they would say. Well, Covid can stop us. "We will make it through." Well, not everyone.

This was the problem revealed: we are needy creatures, and life is far more fragile than we realize. Denying this will do us no good. Trying to motivate ourselves to overcome is sure to run out of steam. For millions of people, Covid meant the death of loved ones, losing their jobs, financial hardship, strained relationships, political strife, church conflict, and persistent despair. (A more honest commercial would have been: "Everything is awful. There's not much to say. But Reese's might help you feel better for a few minutes.")

It is an especially American desire to be autonomous, self-sufficient, and overcoming individuals. We often have far too high a view of ourselves and our abilities. We think *we* will be the generation that will overcome injustice, poverty, bad government, and all other problems. To be "a needy person" is one of the great insults of our performance-based, success-oriented culture.

The bad news is, we won't—and we can't—fix everything. It won't all be dancing children and inspirational music in the end. We are creatures of need. No matter how much money we have, how much security we feel, how much power we have in this life, we're only a microscopic virus away from life-threatening illness. We're only one meeting away from losing our job. We're only a phone call away from the worst day of our life. There will *never* be a time when we are no longer in need.

And believe it or not, that's a good thing. Jesus invites us, commands us, to acknowledge our need and bring it to God.

Why We're Needy Creatures

We are all needy people, and we were created in this way. Being a dependent person isn't a flaw, and it isn't the result of sin and brokenness in the world. Humans were designed by God to be reliant creatures.

Humanity needed God before Adam and Eve sinned, before sin and all its effects entered the world. They needed God for life. They needed God for provision. They needed God's world as a home—a habitat in which they could live, move, multiply, and cultivate good things. And even after sin entered the world, we know that being needy is not the same as being sinful, because even Jesus, in his humanity, experienced need. He relied on his Father's presence—to the point he often withdrew from others to seek it (Matt. 14:23; Luke 6:12; 9:18; Mark 6:46–47). He required food, water, and rest while on earth—to the point that he was so weary and thirsty that he asked a Samaritan woman to give him a drink of water (John 4:6–7). He needed family and friends—to the point that he asked them to stay with him and keep watch in his darkest moments (Matt. 26:38; Luke 22:14–16). Indeed, he was "fully human in every way" (Heb. 2:17), even subject to weakness (Heb. 5:2). At the end of time, all *sin* and *brokenness* will be a distant memory. But *need* will not. For all eternity, we will rely on God's provision, one another, and food and water.

To be human is to be in need. To resist your neediness is to dehumanize yourself and reject God's design. We reject our neediness often out of pride, but also because we have a low view of our physical world, which is the environment by which God meets so many of our needs.

Have you noticed how God leads his people into positions of dependence—only so he can provide for them in miraculous ways? When Israel was in the wilderness for forty years, God hovered over them in a cloud to give them shade (Exod. 13:21–22; 24:15–18). Despite four decades of walking, their sandals didn't wear out, and their clothes didn't get holes (Deut. 29:5). All these years, God provided manna in the wilderness—food that appeared on the ground every morning. They were to collect only what they needed for that day. If they collected any more than was needed for the day, it would spoil (Exod. 16:19–20). Time and again, Israel was surrounded by enemies, or taken into exile, or faced a famine, and when they cried out to God, he brought walls crashing down (Josh. 6), or incited their enemies to wipe each other out (2 Chron. 20:22–23), or provided rain (James 5:17), water (Exod. 17:1–7), and food that never ran out (1 Kings 17:16).

When the Son of God came to earth, he came in need. He didn't descend in glory. He didn't come as a young adult, strong and well-educated and self-sufficient. He came as a baby. He spent nine months in Mary's womb. He was completely dependent on others, like all other babies. He cried. He had his diaper changed. He scraped his knees and needed bandages. He had friends growing up; he learned carpentry from his father; he studied the Scriptures. Luke 2:52 says "he grew in wisdom and stature" as a young man. He was needy and dependent because he was fully human—as well as fully divine. And he didn't just exhibit human neediness. He taught it. In his parables and teachings, Jesus shows us our need. Remember Jesus's Beatitudes? If we could distill them down, they'd be this, simply put: *Blessed are the needy, for they will be satisfied.*

Being a Christian is not primarily about being a good person like Jesus. It's about being the kind of needy, broken person that Jesus loves to forgive and heal and restore. The needy receive

==forgiveness and respond in love==. The proud tragically secure their own future—life without God.

But Jesus doesn't only demonstrate dependence in his own life and speak of it in his teachings. In his healing work, Jesus meets our needs.

Jesus Is Drawn to Your Need

One time in John 5, while going to the temple, Jesus and his friends approach a large group of people with disabilities. One man there had been paralyzed for thirty-eight years. Jesus asks him simply, "Do you want to get well?" (v. 6). It's remarkable that he asks such a basic question. Of course the man wants to be well! Jesus could have just looked at him and instantly healed him. But instead, Jesus draws the man into a conversation. In doing so, he teaches us about our similarly great need for his power and presence. The man mumbles something about not being able to get access to healing—he doesn't even answer the question. Nonetheless, Jesus says to him, "Get up! Pick up your mat and walk" (v. 8). Why would he do this? Because Jesus is drawn to need.

On another occasion recorded in both Mark 5 and Luke 8, Jesus is moving through a crowd, and a synagogue ruler named Jairus approaches him and begs Jesus to heal his only daughter (Luke 8:41–42). Jesus is making his way through the crowd, headed for Jairus's house when a woman with great need interrupts him—she had had a chronic health issue for twelve years—and reaches out to touch Jesus's clothes. Why? Because "when she heard about Jesus, she came up behind him in the crowd and touched his cloak, because she thought, 'If I just touch his clothes, I will be healed'" (Mark 5:27–28). The result? "Immediately her bleeding stopped and she felt in her body that she was freed from her suffering" (v. 29). Instantly, Jesus realizes power has gone out from him and he stops to ask who had touched him. When the woman sees she can hide no longer, and in a moment of great shame, she reveals her condition and approaches Jesus "and fell at his feet and, trembling with fear, told him the whole truth" (v. 33). And—don't miss this—she doesn't do this in private. The crowds are still around. When she falls down in front of Jesus and explains why she is making physical contact with him, we see that *"in the presence of all the people*, she told why she had touched him" (Luke 8:47, emphasis added). She is doing this in front of a massive gathering of people who will look down on her for her uncleanness and neediness. And yet Jesus raises her up out of her shame and says, "Daughter, your faith has healed you. Go in peace and be freed from your suffering" (Mark 5:34).

Now, pause and recognize the difference between these two individuals. Jairus was a man, a respected leader of the synagogue, a pillar of the Jewish community. This woman, who is not named in the story, is likely older, unmarried or widowed, and lacks any social status; even more, she's chronically ill and unclean. Jairus stands at the center of Jewish life with so much influence; this woman cowers outside of it, with none. You'd expect Christ to be more drawn to Jairus's need—after all, healing the daughter of a synagogue ruler would certainly circulate the news of Jesus like wildfire. Not to mention, Jairus isn't the infected one. He's still in good standing before the community. If the aim is ultimately to spread the good news and reveal Jesus as the divine Son of God, pushing past this woman and getting a move on to Jairus's house would be the efficient and effective method for ministry growth. Draw near to the one in good standing—the guy with influence—right?

This woman, on the other hand, is the infected one. When Jesus realizes power has gone out from him, he could have just moved on to the more important ministry with the more important person on his schedule for the day. Why stop? Especially with such a "better" ministry opportunity waiting for him at Jairus's house? And once he discovers the identity of the person who touched him, why address her further? She got what she wanted, after all. Why linger even longer—long enough to call her daughter, and bless her in the sight of the crowd? Because Jesus is drawn to need—*in all its forms and from all kinds of people*. And he can meet more than one at a time. He can be on his way to meeting one and make time to be interrupted by another. So on the days you feel like your need isn't as important as the next person's, remember this woman and tell yourself the truth: Jesus is drawn to need, and he likes when you interrupt him with yours. More than that, he'll bless you for coming to him and telling him the whole truth about your needs.

On still another occasion in Mark 9, Jesus's disciples had been unable to cast a demon out of a young boy. The boy's father explains the situation to Jesus and brings the boy forward. As the boy again begins to suffer from another seizure, Jesus calmly asks the father how long this has been happening. He is not alarmed at the situation, not overwhelmed with the crisis at hand. Instead, he engages the father in a conversation, drawing out the father's great need (and with it, the boy's). The father exclaims, "if you can do anything, have compassion on us and help us" (Mark 9:22 CSB). The father doesn't have great faith—he readily admits his own struggle to believe—but he does have one thing right. He has great need. So Jesus rebukes the evil spirit and raises the boy up, perfectly healed.

Once more, Jesus is drawn to those with great need. Or more accurately, Jesus is drawn to those with a great *awareness* of their need. In fact, Jesus describes his entire reason for coming to earth like this:

> to preach good news to the poor . . .
>   to proclaim release to the captives
> and recovery of sight to the blind,
>   to set free the oppressed,
> to proclaim the year of the Lord's favor.
> (Luke 4:18–19 CSB)

In short, *to help people in great need.* Jesus willingly came to this earth, not only to teach us about our need, not only to creatively, miraculously meet our physical needs. He ultimately came to give his life as a ransom, or a payment, for our greatest need: our sin-debt.

All of these biblical examples I mention above—these stories of human need and Jesus's providing—have a purpose beyond just the instant physical relief of the characters involved. These stories are pointing to a bigger need that Jesus is meeting: our need of forgiveness. It's our ultimate need. We need forgiveness, but God can't just wave off our sin; forgiveness always requires a cost. When you forgive someone's debt, it has a cost, and you absorb the cost. Someone has to pay a debt. And so, the cost of our sin is death. There is no forgiveness without the shedding of blood (Heb. 9:22). Someone has to pay for this sin—that "someone" being us and that payment being our death—but instead of making us do it, God provides for this great need himself.

So Jesus, having never sinned in his life, went innocently like a lamb to the slaughter, he died in our place, he paid our debt, and when it was finished, he rose from the grave on the third day in victory—the ultimate miracle of God's power.

Why must you remember this? Because it helps you see that the first step in spiritual maturity is not necessarily to be like Jesus. The very first step is to be the kind of person that Jesus is drawn to—desperate, willing, believing, hoping, honest, non-pretentious, sincere. People who simply approach him with their need and tell him the whole truth.

The wealthy and religious are often ignored by Jesus in the Gospels. While he always embraces the poor, the sick, and the needy, he often lets the wealthy and religious walk away empty-handed. He is the same Shepherd who leaves the ninety-nine to find the one. But when a wealthy man or religious leader refuses to follow Jesus, Jesus simply lets them walk away and doesn't pursue them. Why? Because they have no need of him. Or more precisely, they have no *awareness* of their need of him. They think they have all that they need. They think they *are* all that they need. Beware the one with no need.

When we come to Jesus with great need, he responds by giving us his full attention. When we muster up all the faith we can, though we struggle to believe, Jesus stands ready to respond. When we realize we can hide no longer, he is ready to embrace us. When we finally tell him the whole truth about ourselves in prayer, he commends our faith and blesses us with his peace.

A Good Father Delights in Meeting His Children's Needs

But you might ask, doesn't God already know all our needs? If so, then why should we spend so much time praying about them?

Jesus anticipated this very question in Matthew 6:8. In fact, he says, "your Father knows what you need before you ask him," as a *motivation* to pray. Why is God's knowledge of our needs a reason we should bring those needs to him? Because prayer is about *relationship*. It's an expression of our position as his child. Of course, he knows what we need: he wants us to *come* to him, to *be* with him.

When my son Jack was younger, he wanted oatmeal for breakfast every morning. But oatmeal is hard for a young child to make. So he asked for help. Of course, we as his parents knew he wanted oatmeal, and we knew he needed help. But we didn't get annoyed every time he asked for it. Imagine if our response to him was, "We already know you need help with the oatmeal and that you want the oatmeal—why in the world would you *ask* us to help you with it? To be involved with it?" Of course we want our child to come to us with his needs—even if we already know about them. He's ours. We love him. Even making oatmeal is an act of relationship. It's an expression of love, and the fact that he would ask us to help him is simply his way of living within the position he has as our child. He sits at the counter and tells us about whatever is on his mind as we make his breakfast. And as our son, he should.

If parents delight in meeting their children's needs in relationship, how much more does our heavenly Father delight in meeting his children's needs? How much more does he want us to use our position as his children to ask for things—to express our needs to him, even if he already knows them?

This is prayer: we bring our life of need to God, specifically and constantly. Where am I getting this? From the Bible. The main form of prayer in the Scriptures, far and away, is *petition*—asking for what we need. It includes other forms of prayer like intercession, adoration, confession, and so on. Those forms of prayer are certainly and vitally important! We cannot undervalue them. But the vast majority of time in prayer that we witness in the Scriptures

What Do You Want?

is spent asking God for help, guidance, protection, and deliverance for oneself, and for all those things in the lives of others. *God wants us to come to him with all that we are and all that we need, no holding back.*

But, here, we might again struggle to come to our Father in prayer. Are we only to bring our needs to God? What if we don't know if our needs are in line with God's will? What if we *want* something but don't necessarily *need* it?

I'm glad you asked. Because believe it or not, now we're getting to the heart of Jesus's teachings on prayer.

What Do You Want Me to Do for You?

Have you ever noticed that Jesus asks a lot of questions? Certainly, many people ask him questions throughout the Gospels (and we'll get to those later). But Jesus himself asks others a surprising number of questions as well. One question in particular stands out. On numerous occasions, Jesus stops someone in their tracks with this simple question: *What do you want?* (Matt. 20:21, 32; Mark 10:36, 51; Luke 18:41).

This question is odd in almost every situation, so what is he doing? This question is worth our full attention in this chapter. If we can understand the power of this simple question from Jesus—that is, if we can discover the power of asking—we'll be one step closer to discovering a life of joy, strength, and intimacy with God through prayer.

In John 1, Jesus has just begun his public ministry and is beginning to select his disciples. Two of John's disciples began to (literally) follow Jesus. Seeing them behind him, Jesus turns and asks the question, "What do you want?" (v. 38). They answer respectfully—they want to see where he's staying, which is likely a way of asking if they can follow him and learn from him for a few days. But don't rush past the simple power of Jesus's question. In fact, it's the first time we read Jesus's own words in the gospel of John. John is very purposeful in the ordering of events and narratives in his gospel, so he may be trying to highlight Jesus's question. Jesus is drawing these two men into their great need of him. He's drawing them to vocalize their desires. He wants them to say exactly what it is they want and need of him. It wouldn't be the only time Jesus asked his followers that very question.

Next, the John 5 story we mentioned a few pages ago bears further reflection. Jesus and his disciples approach a community of sufferers at the pool of Bethesda. It was a gathering place for "the blind, the lame, the paralyzed" (v. 3), and it was believed to have healing powers. Jesus seems to find the man who had been there the longest, a grizzled thirty-eight-year veteran of paralysis. If there's one thing that's clear about this man, it's that he wants to be healed. He is not only disabled—he has chosen a life where he daily sits by a healing pool. And yet, when Jesus stoops down to talk with him, he begins with a question. *"Do you want to get well?"* (v. 6). The man laments that he cannot get to the waters fast enough—someone always gets there ahead of him (v. 7). But Jesus is undeterred. He tells the paralyzed man to get up, pick up his mat, and go home (v. 8). At once, the man was healed (v. 9). The text never says he was healed for his faith, only that he had great need and no one to help him (v. 7). But Jesus knows what he wants and gives it to him anyway.

Another moment is captured in the gospels of Matthew 20 and Mark 10. One day, the disciples James and John, flanked by their mother, approach Jesus. They have a question for him. Jesus responds simply, "What is it you want?" This is a simple and understandable response. But in light of the many times he asks this question, it takes on increased meaning. Again, he is asking his followers to declare exactly what they're asking of him. Their request is selfish and impossible. The brothers and their mother ask for the same thing—that the brothers might reign on Jesus's right and left hand for all eternity. In fact, when the request is on the brothers' lips, they even frame the request by first saying, "We want you to do for us whatever we ask" (Mark 10:35). It's a remarkably self-centered request. But shockingly, Jesus doesn't seem upset by it. He hears out their desires, and simply lets them know he won't answer their request in the way they want him to, and instead he teaches them about humility (Matt. 20:20–27; Mark 10:35–44).

Moments later, Jesus and his disciples are leaving Jerusalem and pass by two blind men sitting along the road, calling out to him. "Lord, Son of David," they twice cry out; "have mercy on us!" Jesus stops and asks them, "What do you want me to do for you?" Of course, it would have been obvious to Jesus, his disciples, the crowd, and anyone reading the passage today: the blind men want to be healed of their blindness! But Jesus intentionally asks the question. So they must verbalize exactly what they most want from Jesus in that moment: "Lord, we want our sight." As soon as they declare their need, "Jesus had compassion on them and touched their eyes. Immediately they received their sight and followed him" (Matt. 20:29–34; Mark 10:46–52; Luke 18:35–43).

In these four examples, Jesus's followers come to him with their desires and their needs. Jesus invites them to name those wants and needs.

In much the same way, Jesus is still asking this question today—of all of us. *What do you want?*

If we can embrace our neediness, we can identify with not only the disciples, but the sick and disabled men and women of the Gospels too. We can find ourselves in the presence of the healing Lord. When we understand our place as needy children of God, suddenly we discover we can ask for whatever we want (not just need)—and we can trust him to answer in a way that serves us best.

So, what are you asking for? What do you want God to do for you through Jesus?

The Wild Teachings of Jesus on Prayer

This simple question—what do you want?—is not all Jesus had to say about asking for our wants and needs. In fact, Jesus's words on asking are among the most common, significant, and scandalous teachings in the Gospels. Consider the remarkable teachings of Jesus on the power of asking him for exactly what we desire and require. (I remember the first time I read through these passages at once, seeing their power when held together; it's safe to say it changed my prayer life forever.)

In his famous Sermon on the Mount teaching (Matt. 5–7), Jesus is reframing how to think about God, life, and true spirituality. It's where he shares his so-called Lord's Prayer. It's also where he speaks with some of his most humorous and vivid language. In the context of prayer and true spiritual life, he says,

> "Which of you, if your son asks for bread, will give him a stone? Or if he asks for a fish, will give him a snake? If you, then, though you are evil, know how to give good gifts to your children, how much more will your Father in heaven give good gifts to those who ask him!" (Matt. 7:9–11)

Jesus's statement is remarkable. If even average parents give their children good gifts, how much more will his perfect and loving and all-powerful Father give us the good things that we ask for! But Jesus is just getting started.

In Luke 18, Jesus tells an unforgettable parable. A poor widow is being mistreated, neglected, or somehow marginalized. She finds a judge with a bit of jurisdiction over her situation, and she presents her case. It seems that the judge throws her case out. Yet she returns. He throws it out again. But she keeps on coming so many times, that finally he relents and gives her justice. What is the purpose of this brief story? As the introduction states, Jesus wants "to show them that they should always pray and not give up" (Luke 18:1).

Now, my favorite example of Jesus's wild teaching on asking comes in Luke 11. Jesus tells us to imagine this scene. You have some dear, old friends show up late at night. You haven't seen them in ages, and you're excited to have them stay with you. But there's a problem: you're out of bread. You have nothing to feed them with. You would love to stay up all night chatting, catching up, and having a good time. But you need bread. And *a lot* of it. What do you do? You go to your neighbor's house and bang on the door. Your neighbor yells at you through the door and goes back to bed. But you want this bread. You need this bread. You bang on the door again, shouting again your desire for some of his bread. What will happen? Your neighbor, not because he's generous or he cares for you, will finally open the door. "Because of your shameless audacity," Jesus says, "he will surely get up and give you as much as you need" (Luke 11:8).

But here's the genuinely funny thing in Jesus's illustration. In Jesus's imaginary encounter, you ask your neighbor for three loaves of bread (v. 5). That's a lot of bread. Who keeps three loaves of bread around? Even with three growing boys that eat like human vacuum cleaners, we typically only buy one, maybe two loaves at a time. Three loaves of bread is just over the top—especially if it's the first century and you don't have a freezer. Now we've arrived at Jesus's point. You can ask for something, no matter how big or small. You don't have to hold back when you're asking God for what you want. I mean, three loaves of bread? That doesn't even make sense, except when we're thinking about God. Apparently, God keeps three loaves in his kitchen. He's a three-loaf God. Jesus's point is the Father's abundant generosity. You can ask him for your daily bread, but you can also ask him for three full loaves in the middle of the night.

These aren't the only examples. Consider these additional statements by Jesus:

> "For everyone who asks receives; the one who seeks finds; and to the one who knocks, the door will be opened." (Matt. 7:8; Luke 11:10)

> "If you believe, you will receive whatever you ask for in prayer." (Matt. 21:22)

> "Therefore I tell you, whatever you ask for in prayer, believe that you have received it, and it will be yours." (Mark 11:24)

These are not just wild teachings on prayer. If they came from anyone but Jesus, we might call them irresponsible. They don't seem balanced. They don't account for unanswered prayer. They may even seem insensitive. (More on all this in a moment.)

Keep in mind that Jesus's promises here are being made quite generally. Jesus is teaching among large crowds. This means we can be confident that they're not just promises for his own twelve disciples or for super Christians or ministry leaders only. Jesus is giving these bold, borderline irresponsible invitations to everyone who calls God their Father.

But what about when Jesus really pulls his disciples aside and talks to them? Does he balance out this asking-and-receiving business with a bunch of caveats and explain-aways?

The Last Supper, or, How to Live in a Brutal World

When someone is near death, they choose their words carefully. Facing their own end, people often have remarkable clarity and passion as they speak with family and friends for the last time. Even when someone doesn't know they're soon to die, their words may carry increased significance. I have lost close friends and even siblings, and when I thought back to the last words we exchanged, they carry profound importance on each occasion.

So it makes sense that we read Jesus's words at the Last Supper with additional weight. In John 13–17, Jesus has gathered his closest friends, the twelve disciples, in an upper room to celebrate the Passover. The moment is thick with significance. Jesus washes their feet. He explains that he is going back to the Father. He prepares them for life without him on earth. He tells them of the coming Holy Spirit. And he prays for them.

Essentially, Jesus is preparing his disciples to live in a brutal world without his physical presence. The world will reject them, and they will face constant affliction for the remainder of their lives. So it's critically important that they learn the importance of asking before he goes to the cross—and ultimately, back to heaven.

During this remarkable evening, he refers to the business of *asking* four times. In this final meal, let's see how balanced he is when he talks about prayer with his closest disciples.

> "I will do whatever you ask in my name, so that the Father may be glorified in the Son. You may ask me for anything in my name, and I will do it." (John 14:13–14)

> "If you remain in me and my words remain in you, ask whatever you wish, and it will be done for you." (John 15:7)

> "You did not choose me, but I chose you and appointed you so that you might go and bear fruit—fruit that will last—and so that whatever you ask in my name the Father will give you." (John 15:16)

> "Very truly I tell you, my Father will give you whatever you ask in my name. Until now you have not asked for anything in my name. Ask and you will receive, and your joy will be complete." (John 16:23–24)

Jesus is literally the least balanced teacher on prayer ever. I mean, there is little-to-no nuance here. He does say, "if you remain in me" and to ask in his name—meaning we must believe in him and ask things of the Father through an abiding relationship with him. But for the children of God, it's just straight ask-and-receive language. How do we learn to live in a brutal world, without the physical presence of Jesus? We learn to ask God for our wants and needs and to expect that he will respond positively.

Returning to the Fatherhood of God

I can already think of several objections our rational minds (and perhaps the skeptics or cynics among us) could be making right now. Is Jesus telling us to ask in a way that is merely transactional? What if this kind of prayer life treats God as a cosmic genie, instead of God Almighty? What if we get addicted to asking for stuff and forget to simply praise God for who he is? What if we end up worshipping the gifts instead of the Giver? Does an emphasis on asking for our wants—especially on the three-loaf level—put us in dangerous territory, like a low-key prosperity gospel?

It will take the remainder of the book to answer these questions fully, but for now, know this. Jesus is describing a vibrant type of life with God. He's describing relationship. Our relationship to God is not transactional at all; it is deeply personal. In each of these Upper Room passages, notice that Jesus never uses the word "God," he only uses the word "Father." Ask and *your Father* will give you. The whole point of this asking business is that we are needy, dependent children in the arms of a loving, almighty Father.

Good parents delight when their children approach them with their wants and needs. Asking-and-receiving is so often at the heart of the parent-child relationship. A young child is in need and cannot provide for herself, so she asks her parents. The parents look on the child with love and affection, and if it is within their ability and also in the best interest of the child, they say yes.

How much more does our heavenly Father delight in our bold asking him! Jesus is begging us, "Look, I know him. He's a really good Father. He has the ability; he has the capacity. And he knows what's in your best interest. Ask for what you want. It doesn't mean you'll get everything right away. But ask and keep asking. And none of these half-a-loaf prayers. You can't ask God for too much!"

Two of Jesus's closest followers (who also happen to be New Testament authors) knew this theme by heart. And they can help us get it more fully into our hearts. John, the apostle of love, writes this:

> We have confidence before God and receive from him anything we ask, because we keep his commands and do what pleases him. (1 John 3:21–22).

And then, Jesus's earthly brother James, writes something similar. (And these are perhaps the primary places we see any sort of caveat to asking God for our wants and needs.)

> If any of you lacks wisdom, you should ask God, who gives generously to all without finding fault, and it will be given to you. But when you ask, you must believe and not doubt, because the one who doubts is like a wave of the sea, blown and tossed by the wind. That person should not expect to receive anything from the Lord. (James 1:5–7)

> You do not have because you do not ask God. When you ask, you do not receive, because you ask with wrong motives, that you may spend what you get on your pleasures. (James 4:2–3)

In each case, Jesus's friends are reiterating his teachings: "If you lack something, ask God and it will be given to you." The only footnotes they give are fairly straightforward. For John, we must keep Jesus's commands and live a life pleasing to him. For James, we must ask with faith, not doubt, and we must ask with right motives. If we are asking for something that will decrease our dependence on God or minimize our relational connection to him, we are not likely to receive it. (In other words, don't ask for something that will mean you require less of God's personal presence in your life.)

Clearly, for John and James, the emphasis is on bold, childlike asking. Our God is an abundant giver. The more we spend time in his presence, the more our asking will come from right motives and a lifestyle of faithfulness to him. But as we mature, we shouldn't find ourselves asking less of God. We should find ourselves passionately asking much more of him.

Now, we'll look at unanswered prayer in a later chapter, but I hope you can feel the weight of Jesus's teachings at this point. I have just done what I tell young preachers not to do: load people up with about fifteen consecutive passages to make a point. But here, I stand by it. We need to feel the cumulative weight of Jesus's unbelievable invitations to *ask*.

Our first impulse should not be to explain his words away. It shouldn't be to add caveats that he and the other New Testament writers don't add. Our first response should be to praise the Father for his abundant, gracious nature. And our second impulse should be, quite simply, to ask and keep on asking.

Consider this simple but profound task: Ask God for twenty things.

Indeed, we might summarize all of Jesus's teachings on prayer with such a simple statement: *Ask the Father and you will receive.*

Father,
You are all-powerful and all-knowing,
and everything you've made is good.
You have made me a creature of need,
and I trust your ways.
Teach me how to live as a dependent child;
I commit my needs to you.
Lord Jesus, teach me to believe your words—
to ask boldly, and to keep on asking.
I know I can only ask with such power through your Son,
through his life, death, and resurrection.
Praise you, Father, and your Son, the Lord Jesus. Amen.

3

Pour Out Your Hearts Like Water

In the introduction, I quoted my friend Todd, who said, "I've been a Christian for decades, but I've never learned to pray." He made that comment about two years ago, but yesterday I sat with him again over coffee. With joy in his eyes, he said, "Boy, our times of prayer have been incredible! God is really moving!" He was talking about a community group gathering the evening before. They had spent about ninety minutes in prayer, taking turns raising hundreds of requests to the Father. (And I don't mean seventy-five minutes of "sharing" requests and fifteen minutes of praying; we don't even share requests anymore; we just encourage people to pray their needs and let others surround them with their own prayers.)

Todd continued, "For the first time, I'm really looking forward to church and community group every week. I can't wait to see what's going to happen." Todd and his friends are discovering the joy, peace, and power of prayer, and it's turning their lives upside down—or maybe right side up.

When we begin to see all that prayer does, it only invites us deeper into the heart of God and emboldens our requests. When we begin to really pour out our hearts like water, as beloved children of God, prayer begins to work in unbelievably powerful ways.

Before we consider how to pour out our hearts in prayer, let's recognize this significant barrier to prayer. We struggle to believe that prayer does anything.

How does this happen? What exactly does prayer do?

What Prayer Does

Prayer welcomes us into the embrace of the Father and retrains us to live from belovedness.

The apostle Paul wrote, "Because of his great love for us, God, who is rich in mercy, made us alive with Christ even when we were dead in transgressions—it is by grace you have been saved" (Eph. 2:4–5). Quite simply, God created us in love, but in our sin, he lost us. In Christ, he comes to get us back. Through the life, death, and resurrection of his Son, God the Father welcomes us into his loving embrace.

This is the central message of Christianity, the gospel. We are made one with Christ, we are filled with the promised Holy Spirit, and we are showered forever with the tender love of the Father. The practice of baptism demonstrates the great gift of salvation: We were dead to sin (under water) and raised to new life (up from the watery "grave"). But it also represents this: We are immersed in the reality of the Father, Son, and Holy Spirit. As we saw in chapter 1, prayer is where we lay hold of this great news. Our Father invites us into his presence, and in prayer, we respond by letting ourselves collapse on him.

But we struggle to believe that God truly loves us, don't we? Maybe we've been too long exposed to the heavy demands of legalistic religion. Or perhaps we've been raised by parents who either rarely showed affection or used excessive affection in manipulative ways—or worse yet, neglected, abused, or gave up on us. Shame can become our operating system. As a result, it's not hard for us to believe the gospel in an intellectual way; we might even be able to describe with remarkable accuracy the doctrines of justification by faith and substitutionary atonement. *But for all our great doctrine about God, are we living in the love of the Father?*

Prayer retrains us, day by day, moment by moment, to believe *and feel* that God loves us. Prayer is the continual practice whereby we enter God's presence, engage in a face-to-face conversation with him, and then reenter the world living in the overflow of his love. Prayer retrains us to live *from* our belovedness, not *for* it. We see our orphan hearts transformed into the hearts of beloved children. As we already explored in chapter 1, we develop a radical security in the love of God.

Everything in the world tries to rob us of the joy of this belovedness. The world tells us we are the center of the universe and can be and do anything if we just set our minds to it. Because of that, the fate of the world and all its problems is on our shoulders to carry. And when we can't carry it, when we can't fix it or make it perfect, the world then tells us we are failures, we are disappointments, we should be ashamed of ourselves. But this isn't the voice of the

Father. As Henri Nouwen writes, "The truth, even though I cannot feel it right now, is that I am the chosen child of God, precious in God's eyes, called the Beloved from all eternity, and held safe in an everlasting belief."[1]

Nouwen is encouraging us to a healthy self-talk, to prayerfully remind ourselves of who God has made us to be, to reject the lies of the enemy and the joy-theft of the world, and to fully embrace the belovedness that the gospel welcomes us into.

Prayer uncovers our divided lives and enables wholehearted living.

In the presence of our good and perfect God, we experience his tender love but also are confronted by our own brokenness. This is where many of us are tempted to stop in prayer. Prayer exposes us. It confronts us with our true nature. Our lives are divided and dishonest. We love God and the world; we hide our motivations and cover up our actions to save face; we share half-truths and project the most beautiful versions of ourselves on social media.

But there is a grace here too. Our devotions are not wholly centered on God, and the truth terrifies us. Our sins are forgiven in Christ, but still, we live with this sinful nature. Further, we are beset by temptations of the world and the attacks of the enemy. But prayer reveals our reality and teaches us the freedom of confession.

When we truly embrace our belovedness, we are free to bring our divided lives and sinfulness before God with a total honesty. Confessing our sins becomes a delight. As the late pastor and author Jack Miller used to say, "Spiritual maturity doesn't mean we repent less, it means we repent faster."[2]

As we confess our sins to our good and loving Father in prayer, he softens our hearts and allows us to live from great security in his approval in and affection for us. Prayer gives us space to imagine a new way of living. Psalm 86 teaches us to pray,

> Teach me your way, LORD,
>   that I may rely on your faithfulness;
> give me an undivided heart
>   that I may fear your name. (v. 11)

It is a mercy of God to reveal our inner dividedness and call us to wholeness. This, in fact, is what he has promised he will do through his Holy Spirit. "I will give them an undivided heart," he says through the prophet Ezekiel, "and put a new spirit in them; I will remove from them their heart of stone and give them a heart of flesh" (11:19). Prayer welcomes us into this mature, wholehearted living.

Prayer enables us to face pain and suffering with honesty and hope.

Praying with joy and power doesn't always feel like praying with joy and power. Often, prayer is simply coming before God when we feel like doing anything else. The weight of life in a broken world rests heavy on our shoulders. The losses of fractured relationships, failed dreams, and unmet expectations call us to just stay in bed. What good is prayer anyway?

But Jesus's prayer and the Psalms encourage us: prayer is not where we set our griefs and hurt aside and press through. We say this at our church all the time: "Don't leave your stresses and worries at the door; bring them inside. And then give them to the Father."

==Lament is the biblical form of prayer that lifts our weary souls and burning frustrations to God.== We literally unload on him, and he welcomes it. Are you angry about something? Let him know. Do you feel like he's distant? Tell him. Are you disappointed, bored, or just plain unhappy? He can handle it. Lament is God's invitation to bring our complaints to God.

Roughly one-third of all the Psalms are laments, and many of the other Psalms include moments of lament as well. I suspect this will be true of our prayers as well. Somewhere around one-third of our prayers will simply be laments:

> Father, how long will I have to deal with this sickness?

> Lord, my relationship with my son is such a mess—please help!

> God, I can't feel your presence at all. Where are you?

> Lord, my friend is suffering greatly. Why aren't you doing anything?

> Father, all I can feel is depression and anxiety and I don't want to pray. The end.

But if the official prayer book of the Bible (the Psalms) embraces this pattern, shouldn't we as well? Bring your greatest fears and deepest heartache to the Father. As Peter says, "Give all your worries and cares to God, for he cares about you" (1 Pet. 5:7 NLT). As we raise our laments to God and thank him for his presence with us, we gain fresh courage to face the most difficult parts of our lives.

Prayer opens us to a life of celebration and thanksgiving and teaches us to praise.

Something remarkable happens in lament, though; I have to warn you. Our complaints are received by God, and we are transformed. Just listen to his promises: "Cast your cares on the Lord and *he will sustain you*" (Ps. 55:22, emphasis added).

When we sit in the presence of our Father-King, lament turns to praise and thanksgiving. We move from complaining to celebration. In the all-consuming *sanctuary* (presence) of God, our perspective changes and we are overwhelmed with gratitude and trust (Ps. 73).

Much has been said and written about the power of gratitude. Its powers are well-documented in modern-day studies, talk show episodes, and podcasts. But the Psalter is the original book of gratitude. Thanksgiving fills the pages of our Psalms, and they're often intermingled with laments and intercession and praise.

And like the Psalms, our prayer lives can hold lament and celebration in tension. We don't have to choose sadness or happiness, grief or joy. In prayer, we can hold it all together. We can honestly pour out our pains and complaints before the Father, and we can receive his peace and joy with gratitude. We can bring real pain to God and leave with real joy—and not feel bad about it. Prayer paves the way for celebration and opens us to praise God through the stuff of life—not around it.

Prayer connects us to other believers more deeply and the mission of God more fruitfully.

We cannot learn to pray alone. Most of our prayers will be in private (as we saw in the first chapter, Jesus teaches us to go into our prayer closets and close the door), but one major way we learn to pray is by praying with others. I have learned *about* prayer through many biblical narratives and dozens of great books on the topic. But I have learned *to* pray by praying alongside godly women and men who are seasoned in their prayer journeys.

We learn by praying with others and we also learn by praying *for* others—the ministry of intercession. The more you develop a life of prayer, the more connected you will be to the lives of your friends, neighbors, family members, and fellow churchgoers.

These two practices—praying with and for others—connect us to one another more deeply. Think of two churches. The first congregation has great music, dynamic teaching, and engaging ministry programs, but its prayer life is sporadic and superficial. The second congregation lacks impressiveness in production and programs, but its members have established more than twenty monthly gatherings for prayer and worship. They're constantly in prayer. You can't stop them from praying. Now, which congregation do you think experiences greater fellowship and unity? The second, of course!

This is almost universally true: Praying churches have remarkable unity, connection, fellowship, and mission alignment. Because they're living before the face of God, praying for and with one another, and seeking first the good of others and the growth of the kingdom. It's possible, I'm guessing, to achieve great church unity without prayer. But why would we neglect this God-given resource for fellowship and unity? Prayer connects us like nothing else.

Prayer increases our experience of the Holy Spirit's presence and power.

As those who know me or attend the church where I pastor can attest, I can only go so long without mentioning the indwelling power of the Holy Spirit! How do we lay hold of the truths of the gospel, the love of the Father, and the way of Jesus? The Holy Spirit. How do we get the love of the Father and the Son into our hearts? There's a Person of the Trinity for that.

Consider the book of Acts again. Throughout the first thirty years after Jesus's ascension, the church expanded from a couple hundred believers in Jerusalem to hundreds of thousands on three different continents. And yet these were the same uneducated, ordinary women and men from the Gospels. What changed? They became indwelt and empowered by the Holy Spirit! In Acts, we see the early believers continuing the ministry of Jesus in the power of the Spirit. They preached the good news of the kingdom. They encouraged the poor and needy and challenged the religious leaders of the day. They healed the sick, restored the blind, cast out demons, and even raised the dead. And on nearly every page of Acts, the Spirit is present. He is living and active, and he is often speaking and directing the believers. Later, the apostles explained to the Thessalonians that their message came "not simply with words but also with power, with the Holy Spirit and deep conviction" (1 Thess. 1:5).

The Holy Spirit is our secret superpower for prayer. He takes all that Christ has said and impresses it upon our hearts. He takes the truths from our minds and delivers them to our hearts. Throughout this book, I hope you'll see the wonder and gentle power of the Spirit of God to enliven us in prayer. Without a truly trinitarian prayer life, we'll always lack the joy and power of prayer that is available to us.

Prayer reorients us to eternity—the coming new creation.

Prayer reminds us that this life is but a breath (Ps. 39:5). Our days are like a fleeting shadow (Ps. 144:4). Our lives are "a mist that appears for a little while and then vanishes" (James 4:14). Now, that doesn't mean our lives don't matter. But rather, in comparison to our eternal lives, in comparison to the coming new creation, this earthly life is so temporary. Prayer—as my friend Scotty Smith once put it—is smelling the grass of the new creation.

How so? Prayer is simply communion with God, and communing with God is exactly what we'll be doing for all eternity in all sorts of ways. And anything we'll be doing for all eternity is certainly worth giving ourselves to now.

Prayer lifts us out of the grind of this broken world. It reorients us to what's eternal. In doing so, it gives us a heavenly perspective. Even more, it gives us increased motivation for bringing the power of the new creation back into our own neighborhoods and workplaces.

To put it simply, *prayer does stuff.*

Some of it is a mystery. I don't pretend to know *how* prayer does all that it does. But it doesn't do nothing, that's for sure.

Now, we're getting ready for prayer. We have learned to receive the Father's embrace. We have released our insecure, performing spirituality with a childlike faith. We have embraced our needs and are ready to bring our heart's desires to the Father. And we have rediscovered just how much prayer really does. What now? Now, we pour out our hearts in prayer. Indeed, we were designed to do just this.

Our Hearts Were Made to Be Poured Out

Julia Cameron's *The Artist's Way* has been credited with helping thousands of writers and artists discover their creative potential. Her unique practices and rituals are aimed at clearing the distractions and false narratives that limit our imaginative capacities. Cameron suggests we begin each day with a simple but time-consuming practice called "morning pages." We all wake up with clutter and fear and voices of accusation in our minds, she says, and we simply cannot be productive creatively until we've let them out. Take three sheets of paper, then, and fill them with whatever words and sentences come to mind. The point is not to end up with some paragraphs or stories that might become useful later in the day. No, you just throw the papers out when you're done. The goal is simply an uncluttered mind. Writing whatever is on your mind—most likely, it's fears and burdens and heartache—brings about a sense of peace. This exercise has been incredibly helpful for me before writing, but even more, I've found it shows us something true of ourselves. We are naturally anxious, busy-minded people, and we can only find inner peace by pouring out these thoughts.

Thankfully, when it comes to praying to the Father, we don't just pour these thoughts onto a legal pad sheet and then throw them out. We pour them out to our living, loving, listening God. He hears us. He receives our random and wild outpourings. And he responds by pouring joy, peace, and strength back into our hearts.

The Old Testament prophets and songwriters knew this intuitively. There's something innately healing about letting our thoughts, emotions, and words overflow. Our hearts were made to be poured out.

Think of David, the psalmist and man after God's own heart. Though he was Israel's great king, David was no stranger to rejection, loneliness, grief, and persecution. David was a man acquainted with sorrows and spent long stretches of his life in isolation. Before he lived in his lush palace in Jerusalem, he spent his time in caves and in the wilderness. His psalms speak out of the overflow of his own need, but they also reveal the heart of God for all time. David made this appeal centuries ago:

> My salvation and my honor depend on God;
>   he is my mighty rock, my refuge.
> Trust in him at all times, you people;
>   *pour out your hearts to him,*
>   for God is our refuge.
> (Ps. 62:7–8, emphasis added)

Think also of Jeremiah, the weeping prophet who spent his life in exile. His prophetic ministry caused him to lose friends, status, and stability. He had few followers, and his message was rejected by his contemporaries. Out of his great struggle, Jeremiah invoked David's imagery to call the struggling Israelites back to God in the midst of their great suffering:

> Arise, cry out in the night,
>   as the watches of the night begin;
> *pour out your heart like water*
>   *in the presence of the Lord.*
> Lift up your hands to him
>   for the lives of your children,
> who faint from hunger

at every street corner.
(Lam. 2:19, emphasis added)

Could there be a more wonderful invitation to prayer?

As God's children, full of desire and need, we can enter the Father's presence and unload everything weighing down our busy lives and minds. That's prayer. It's releasing our anxieties once more. It's casting our burdens on him, because we know he cares for us (1 Pet. 5:7). Even more, we know he can carry our burdens.

Further, God (through David and Jeremiah) is not just an inviting us to pour out our hearts during times of special need, great suffering, or incredible loss. He welcomes us to himself every moment of every day. We can *live* in a place of heart-pouring prayer.

Before we dive into this phrase, let's review for a moment. We have already discussed our status as God's children, and we've discussed the turn from an anxious spirituality to childlike dependence. We have seen our great need of God and others, and we've heard Jesus's invitation to ask him for what we want and need. All of this is important to hold in mind as we come to the Lord's welcome to pour out our hearts before him.

So now, let's look at this phrase, but I want to do so in reverse order: *in the presence of the Lord, like water, your hearts pour out.*

In the Presence of the Lord

We begin with the Lord's presence as a way of remembering who our God is. Come into the throne-room of God; enter his courts with thanksgiving. Approach your Father with boldness. Come directly to the King and let him know what's on your heart. Perhaps you're struggling again with this image. Can we really approach God so boldly? Well, remember who you are.

When President Obama was serving his first term, he was a rare president to have young children in the White House while in office. I remember seeing a picture of his two daughters sitting on his lap and climbing on him in between meetings in the Oval Office. There was one of the world's most powerful individuals, sitting at his stately desk, surrounded by legislators and staff members . . . and being climbed upon by two rowdy children. If the girls were anything like my children, he'd be covered in peanut butter, cereal crumbs, and juice residue for the rest of the day.

No matter how hard I tried, I could not get this kind of access to the president. Maybe if I went to law school, worked my way up in public service, received a job on the administration staff (all of which would still make my chances one in a million, not to mention my high school stats were nothing impressive)—maybe then I could stand in the back of the oval office to witness a five-minute meeting between important people. But these two girls did none of that. They hadn't even finished grade school! How did they get access to the president? Easy. They were his children.

This is a wonderful picture, because the same is true for us. Imagine the God of the universe, sitting on his throne in the heavenly realms. But in between ruling the cosmos and defeating Satan, sin, and death, we knock at the door. The voice in our mind might tell us, "No one can approach the almighty God, are you crazy?" But instead, the door flings open, we are ushered in, and our Father leaps off his throne and runs to embrace us.

We are invited, welcomed, called, and summoned to enter into the presence of the Lord. Not because we worked our way into it, but simply because we're his children. We don't have to make the journey to the temple. We don't have to collect our sins and wait for a priest to be in office. We don't have to wait till Sunday morning.

Right here, right now, God invites us into his presence. He knows what we need before we do, and what we need is him. This is why nearly every psalm calls God our help, our refuge, our rest, our mighty fortress, or some other image of strength and security. We need him, and he welcomes us to come, even now. To come and pour our hearts out like water.

Like Water

Think of the act of pouring water. Each morning, I fill my oversized mason jar with filtered water before filling up the coffee maker. Later, I might go around gently watering the plants around the house from the same jar. In the evening, I might water the lawn from a garden hose. In each act, I'm not measuring exactly or too worried about the ounces and size of the container. To pour water gives the impression of abundance and overflow.

So why do the psalmist and prophets call us to pour out our hearts *like water*? Perhaps they want to show us something of the nature of our prayers. Rather than a slow, careful reciting of words, our prayers can be the natural, unfiltered overflow of our hearts and minds. When we are bursting at the seams with the worries and demands of this life, God has given us a release valve. When we are full, we can pour out.

Nothing is simpler and more basic than water. When milk is poured out, some color will remain. When wine is poured out, a smell remains. When soda is poured out, sticky sugar remains. But when water is poured out? Nothing remains. In the same way, when we pour out our hearts *like water*, he receives it all and no burdens remain. All has been given to him; all will be carried by him.

And there's another side to this: when we pour out, God pours out on us too. God's blessing also flows like water. He is the God of abundance and overflow. As the self-replenishing source of life, our Father pours out his own goodness and peace, even as we pour out our hearts like water before him. God's blessing being poured into us happens simultaneously to our pouring out our hearts in his presence. The weak pouring out anxiousness, confusion, and need, and the strong pouring out love, strength, and blessing in response—all like water.

And just as water fills the lowest places in a jar first, so too God's blessing tends to come to those who need it most. The humblest, lowest hearts receive God's refreshment first. This is another reminder to pursue humility in his kingdom. The lowest places get filled first. Have the lowliness of heart to pour out your prayers like water, and God will pour out his presence like water as well.

Your Hearts

We're not just pouring out prayers though, we're pouring out our very hearts. In the Scriptures, the heart is not merely the place of feeling or emotion. It includes that, but it's deeper. In both Old and New Testaments, the heart is the center of our being; it's the core and sum of who we are. It's the truest, deepest part of us. This is why the Proverbs says, "Above all else, guard your heart, for everything you do flows from it" (Prov. 4:23). And it's why both Moses and Jesus say the summary of religious life is to "love the LORD your God with all your heart" (Deut. 6:5; Matt. 22:37).

And yet the question of Jeremiah 17:9 rings true: "Who can understand [the heart]?" Our hearts can remain largely hidden from us. We barely understand why we do what we do and why certain things just pour out of our mouths. Prayer is a way of discovering (or rediscovering) our own hearts. Even more, it's a way that God reshapes our hearts. It's how God makes our hearts more like Christ's heart.

As we give our hearts to God in prayer, we are giving him the core and essence of our lives. We are giving ourselves completely to him. "Don't give your heart away," the saying goes, assuming that no one can be fully trusted with our whole hearts. God alone can satisfy our hearts and grow them at once. Only God can protect our hearts and use the heartaches of life to mature and strengthen our hearts.

Pour Out

In my earlier examples of filling my mason jar and watering the plants, the pouring of water was imprecise and yet still fairly controlled. But have you seen a *child* pour water? Have you nervously watched as a little one attempts to fill her cereal bowl with milk from a full gallon jug? Even a child can pour something, but it's often a messy, sticky process—sometimes resulting in an ever-expanding puddle of milk on the kitchen floor.

This is the image God has chosen to give us for our praying lives. Just pour it out. Let it flow. Don't hold back. Spills and messes will happen, and there will be days when we feel like a puddle on the floor. But God's welcome is simple: Pour it out.

This is why the Psalms are so helpful. They're brutally honest. They are full of anger, complaints, and demands. Some of them are a little dramatic: "It's been a waste that I have kept my heart blameless; I'm still punished every day anyways" (Ps. 73:13–14, author paraphrased). Others call on God to ruthlessly destroy their enemies. And Psalm 88 seems utterly hopeless as it ends without resolution or peace: "darkness is my closest friend." If someone prayed one of these prayers at our Friday night prayer gatherings, we'd be concerned and refer them to pastoral care. So why are these raw, emotional prayers included in God's Word? Because they demonstrate real people honestly wrestling with God and (usually) praising him in the end.

The Psalms are God's way of saying: Let it all out. Don't hold back. Don't try to be "fairly controlled." Don't make sure you sanitize your prayers. Your prayers can't be too honest for God; he knows what's going on in your heart already. Charles Spurgeon writes:

> You to whom his love is revealed, reveal yourselves to him. His heart is set on you, lay bare your hearts to him. Turn the vessel of your soul upside down in his secret presence, and let your inmost thoughts, desires, sorrows, and sins be poured out like water. Hide nothing from him, for you *can* hide nothing. To the Lord, unburden your soul. . . . To keep our griefs to ourselves is to hoard up wretchedness. The stream will swell and rage if you dam it up; give it a clear course, and it leaps along and creates no alarm.[3]

Give the Lord your everything; he can handle it. We don't have to hold it all together and keep it clean. We don't have to do this life in our own strength. God wants to give us his joy, peace, and strength. And he desires to pour these gifts into us through prayer. Our job is to empty ourselves first, so that we might have ample room to receive them.

My wife, Jessie, recently described a conversation between two counselors on a podcast she follows. One counselor stated that the Covid pandemic had been difficult for everyone, but in all different ways. For some, it meant grief over the death of loved ones; for others, it meant exhaustion from constant parenting and homeschooling; others still were most anxious about unemployment and finances. The only thing that everyone had in common during the height of the pandemic was that we were all living at a reduced capacity. We were all struggling, and we needed the help of our friends and family. And yet the people we needed help from had no help to give—because their capacity was diminished as well.

The counselors then stated that there was no self-replenishing source of help and strength in the world. There's nowhere we can go, they said, and always get filled back up. We must do it ourselves.

You have likely felt this sentiment, even if you haven't had the exact words for it. When it gets hard, there's nowhere to turn. Everyone else is just as overwhelmed, anxious, and "tapped out" as we are. It's up to us, then, to turn it around, pull it together, and climb out of the hole.

As Christians, though, we have a not-so secret resource. We *do* have a self-replenishing source of strength and refuge. He is the spring of living water (Jer. 2:13). He has life in himself; he has no needs (John 5:26). He never sleeps, and he never tires (Ps. 121:4). And even better, he is compassionate, gracious, and generous. He wants to give us his strength and peace.

As Psalm 55 says in Eugene Peterson's paraphrase, "Pile your troubles on God's shoulders—he'll carry your load, he'll help you out" (v. 22 MSG). Or as Jesus put it himself, "Come to me, all of you who are weary and carry heavy burdens, and I will give you rest" (Matt. 11:28 NLT).

Our hearts were made to be poured out. Your ever-loving Father waits for you to bring all your rants and ramblings to him. "Come to me," he says, in essence, "and pour out your hearts like water. And I will give you my peace."

———

Father,
Thank you that you have not left us alone in the world.
You love us and call us sons and daughters.
We have not earned and worked our way in,
but we enter without hesitation as your beloved children.
We struggle to believe in all that prayer does;
show us your power through prayer.
Teach us—retrain our hearts—
to pour out our hearts before you.
Grant us your peace and rest, good God,
and make us more like yourself in the end.
In Christ, the way and the life,
Amen.

4

Heart-at-Rest Prayer

We live in a world with more noise than any generation before us. Centuries ago, humans lived in relative quiet. Sounds came mostly from nature and other living creatures: the whistling of birds, the leaves rustling in the wind, the sounds of animals on a nearby farm. But in our modern age, we are surrounded by incessant (and many times, blaring) man-made noise and barely realize it. In fact, our bodies are so hard-wired for quiet that noise often triggers a defensive physical response. This is helpful if a predator is approaching or a storm is forming over us, but it also means our bodies may be running on high alert without us realizing it. Further, research has shown that noise adversely affects our attention, memory, learning, and interactions with others. Even worse, constant exposure to noise elevates our stress levels, causes anxiety, and is associated with increased rates of heart disease.[1]

Quite simply, noise is killing us.

It shouldn't surprise us, then, that research also points to the healing potential of silence. In fact, two hours of quiet at home has been shown to increase the production of new brain cells, especially those that help regulate our mood. Even just two minutes of silence has been shown to lead to greater stress relief than other relaxation techniques.²

Consider doing that now: I give you permission to set this book down, turn off the music, and just sit quietly. Most likely, there's man-made noise around you beyond your control (not to mention plenty of *human* noise if you have kids or roommates at home). But take just two minutes to sit quietly and notice the noise around you. Pretty remarkable, right?

Now, we consider a second challenge to prayer. How do we find quiet in a world where we are surrounded, inundated, and consumed by hurry and noise? A life of prayer depends upon the cultivation of silence and solitude.

Here, we expose the barriers to a life of quiet and invite one another to an inward deepening of faith. With the false promises of insecure, performative spirituality exposed, we can move deeper into the posture of the beloved child. But old habits—hurry, living in noise, and constantly digesting new content—must be released. And new habits must be embraced. Through daily silence and solitude, we find an anchor for our souls.

Compulsive is a fair word to describe our modern culture. I'll speak at least to my own experience in middle-class America: We are a driven, busy, and restless people. We compulsively check our iPhones and scroll through Netflix; we compulsively speed between meetings and kids' activities with fast-food wrappers scattered on the floor; we compulsively try to keep up with others, projecting an image of balance, passion, and lightheartedness. It's not so much that we want to have it all; we want to do it all. We want to *be* it all. I wouldn't be the first to suggest this American compulsiveness is spreading like a virus in the church too. In my experience, church people are busier, more hurried, and more overloaded than my non-churchgoing friends. After all, we have church responsibilities and relationships to manage on top of work, family, vacations, social media, and youth sports.

It's as if Jesus's piercing question was meant specifically for the twenty-first-century American church: "What good is it for someone to gain the whole world, yet forfeit their soul?" (Mark 8:36).

Jesus moved at his own pace, to say the least. It's not that he wasn't busy—his schedule was full, and he seems to be managing a few hundred relationships in the Gospels. But he wasn't hurried. He was present. Most of all, he let his activity be the overflow of his stillness. His words were the result of his silence. The power of his relationships flowed from the depth of his solitude.

In prayer, the Father is offering us an opportunity to slow down, be silent, and find ourselves in relationship to his holy and perfect nature. Tim Keller has framed contemplative prayer as "heart-at-rest prayer." He wrote that "the goal of contemplation is a heart engagement with the cognitive truth you have been reflecting on. It can be fleeting or sustained, light or pronounced. Its essence is an adoring gaze at God . . . a wordless gazing on and admiration of the Lord."[3] But before we can reach a place of heart-at-rest prayer, we'll have to enter into a quiet that will enable such depth.

Finding Our Quiet

There's more noise in our lives than actual sound. We're addicted to the "noise" of constant feedback. We are trained to live on the praise of others, the approval of our peers, and the perception of our success and goodness. In 1981, spiritual writer Henri Nouwen wrote, "Our society is not a community radiant with the love of Christ, but a dangerous network of domination and manipulation in which we can easily get entangled and lose our soul."[4] How much truer is that four decades later?

Over the last few decades, the evangelical church in America has made an important call to influence the broader society with the good news about Jesus. This witness may include taking roles in civic leadership, serving within major institutions, and starting businesses and non-profits. I thank God for this and encourage my church members to do all this.

But the risk in seeking to change the culture is that the culture can easily change us. Amid our busy activities, we believers are prone to living quite secular lives—lives built around the values of the world. That is, our lives don't look notably different from non-Christians. In my pastoral experience, church attendees are just as prone to overworking, living in anxiety, spending beyond our budget, and protecting our own comfort and security as anyone outside the church. We want to succeed, to raise well-mannered honor roll students, and to have a house so nice we always remark "it was really a gift from the Lord." We want to have it all, whatever "it" is. Despite a relationship with God and regular church attendance, the pace and worry of our lives can lead us to become anxious and prayerless people.

Apart from a deep, abiding prayer life, we struggle to find our identity in Christ. Although we are in Christ—irrevocably joined to him through his life, death, and resurrection—we functionally live as if our identity has to be decided, pursued, and defended on our own. If we are not immersed in the constant affirmation of our Father, we will maintain a gnawing need for the affirmation of others. Henri Nouwen described this need poignantly.

> Who am I? I am the one who is liked, praised, admired, disliked, hated or despised. Whether I am a pianist, a businessman or a minister, what matters is how I am perceived by my world. If being busy is a good thing, then I must be busy. If having money is a sign of real freedom, then I must claim my money. If knowing many people proves my importance, I will have to make the necessary contacts. The compulsion manifests itself in the lurking fear of failing and the steady urge to prevent this by gathering more of the same—more work, more money, more friends.[5]

I resonate deeply with this diagnosis. Even though my identity is secure and I am living from the Father's affirmation and love, performative spirituality raises its ugly head again. I fall back into my old ways of striving and defending and proving. What is the antidote to this compulsive need for others' praise and approval? A life of silent prayer.

It is fitting that silence and solitude often go together. When we are alone, we can finally experience true quiet. When we are in a silent place, more than likely we are enjoying solitude and recovering our energy.

Being alone is nearly unbearable for some people, either by personality or learned need of others. My middle son is so relational and extroverted that he hates being alone for more than a few minutes. This isn't a flaw in his personality; he just loves being with others. But for many of us, we need far more silence and solitude than we realize. It's in solitude that we experience great struggle and great breakthrough. We struggle against the wild thoughts and emotions that rise to the surface. And we experience the calming presence of God calling us to himself. We literally break through from self-centeredness into God-centeredness in silence and solitude.

Why is silence so terrifying? When we are quiet and still and alone, we lose so much of what normally gives us a sense of safety and security. We feel safe when we're busy—at least we're doing something, we think. We feel secure when others are with us—at least they can validate us. We feel strong when we are active—this meeting or action gives me a sense of purpose and meaning. Nouwen considers all this our "scaffolding."[6] Like the framework we install around a building when constructing or renovating it, we put up such things around our lives too. We surround ourselves with music, podcasts, coworkers, friends, TV, and pets to protect us from the gnawing silence within.

When we take down our scaffolding for a moment, when we must truly face ourselves, it can feel terrifying and unsafe. Prayer is often most challenging because we must face ourselves honestly. Silence exposes our preference for noise. Stillness is uncomfortable because of our need for activity. Solitude feels like loneliness when we're accustomed to being surrounded by others.

Further, when we do reach a place of quiet, anxiety may rise up within us as soon as we start praying. As Tyler Staton points out, prayer can actually make us more anxious.[7] When life is busy and noisy, we can tune out the anxiousness and insecurity of our souls.

But when we turn it all off, shut it down, and lock ourselves in a quiet room, all the wild monkeys of our mind come to life.

The task is to persist in silence and solitude until the wild monkeys of our thoughts finally tire and sit down. When all the interrupters have given up and gone home, we can finally enjoy the peace and quiet. But it's here that we must face ourselves, discover what's truly going on in our hearts and minds and bodies, and connect with the still, soft voice of God. If we can become comfortable with silence and solitude, we'll develop a capacity for God's words to take root in us.

Throughout the Scriptures, we see the importance of finding quiet spaces to pray and seek God. The Scriptures, in fact, also equate quiet with a posture of trust and waiting (Isa. 30:15). The two go together: when we find quiet places to reconnect with our heavenly Father, we can hear his voice and learn to trust him in patient waiting again.

Over the remaining six chapters, I'll introduce (or reacquaint you with) nine classic forms of prayer. There are surely more than nine, but I have found that these practices enable us to engage with the Father in important and transformative ways. Consider these nine ways to pour out your heart.

In this chapter, I want to present three practices for a heart at rest—adoration, contemplation, and confession.

Practice #1: Reorienting to God (Adoration)

Remember, Jesus's disciples asked a lot of bad questions, so when they asked him to teach them to pray, he was delighted (Luke 11:1). So, with his disciples (and an eager crowd) gathered on the mountainside one afternoon, Jesus taught them to pray.

The words that followed are among the most famous words ever spoken: "Our Father which art in heaven, Hallowed be thy name" (Matt. 6:9 KJV).

The Lord's Prayer is rightly understood to be the most important prayer for Christians, but it's even more than that. Tertullian called it a summary of the gospel. Thomas Watson called it a body of divinity. J. I. Packer believed it to be "a key to the whole business of living," adding, "What it means to be a Christian is nowhere clearer than here."[8]

The Lord's Prayer is only fifty-three words in my English translation and can be learned and recited easily by a child. But let's not be misled by its brevity or familiarity. The prayer is a vision for life in the inbreaking kingdom of Christ. It's an acknowledgment of the injustice, hunger, and evil of this broken world. It's a statement of faith, it's a call to worship, and it's a battle cry. It's a bold pleading for divine glory, social renewal, and heaven-on-earth transformation.

Packer writes, "Every word of the Lord's Prayer reflects the Lord's vision of what our lives should be—unified, all-embracing response to the love of our heavenly Father, so that we seek his glory, trust his care, and obey his word every moment of every day."[9] Thus, the structure of the Lord's Prayer is a great pattern for our daily prayers.

How, then, does Jesus open his all-important prayer? With praise and adoration. If the Lord's Prayer opens with praise, it's because Jesus wants us to (primarily) begin our prayers with praising God for who he is. This simple act will serve to reorient our hearts and make us more like Christ.

This form of prayer is classically called *adoration*—the business of praying our praise. Of course, Jesus begins the prayer with our posture (just like we did in the first chapter): "Our Father in heaven" (Matt. 6:9). But he then immediately follows it with a word of praise: "hallowed be your name." What does this mean? "Hallowed" is a form of the word "holy"; it comes from the King James Version but is left in most modern translations. In this single word, two things are present: a truth and a call to action. The *truth* is that God is holy, unique, and glorious. The *call to action* is that we would praise, elevate, honor, identify with, meditate upon, and submit to God. And to praise God's "name" is to praise his character, his essence; it's to praise him simply for who he is.

Packer writes, "Lesson one is to grasp that God matters infinitely more than we do."[10] If that's lesson one (the truth), then lesson two (the call to action) is that we must reorient ourselves around that truth. To pray "Hallowed be your name" is to say, like Psalm 115:1, "Not to us, but to your name be the glory."

While this reorientation is a significant and ongoing challenge, it's also a return to how we were designed to live. We are hard-wired for praise. When we experience something great, we cannot contain it. We want to share it, to glory in it, and to invite others into this thing. When a baby is born, the parents want nothing more than to share the news, post a picture, show off that baby. When someone accomplishes something great, he'll want to boast about it.*

Hallowing the name of the Lord is an act of praise. We see something that overwhelms us—his beauty, truth, goodness, justice, glory—and we want to participate in it and share it with others. We're made for this. Hallowed is the name of the Lord, therefore we pray and sing and we live, "Hallowed be your name."

---

*There was a guy on my cycling team this week that completed something incredible. But he's super-humble so he won't go on and on about it. Maybe in his Sunday sermon, but not in a prayer book.

Be who you are God—not who we want you to be. Hallowed be your name—let everyone see your holiness; may your kingdom come on earth as it is in heaven. You are holy and good and right—and we commit our way to following you. Your will be done, not ours.

This pattern is not original to Jesus. Have you noticed how many psalms begin with this important posture?

> Lord, our Lord, how majestic is your name in all the earth! (Ps. 8:1)

> I will exalt you, Lord, for you lifted me out of the depths. (Ps. 30:1)

> Sing joyfully to the Lord, you righteous; it is fitting for the upright to praise him. (Ps. 33:1)

> I will sing of the Lord's great love forever. (Ps. 89:1)

> Sing to the Lord a new song; sing to the Lord, all the earth. (Ps. 96:1)

> Praise the Lord, my soul; all my inmost being, praise his holy name. (Ps. 103:1)

> Give thanks to the Lord, for he is good. His love endures forever. (Ps. 136:1)

By my count, sixty-seven of the 150 Psalms begin with a verse of praise.* In fact, fourteen psalms begin with the same three

---

*In addition to the psalms above, see also Psalms 9, 18, 19, 21, 24, 27, 29, 33, 34, 44, 46, 47, 48, 62, 63, 65, 66, 73, 75, 76, 81, 82, 84, 87, 88, 90, 91, 92, 93, 95, 97, 98, 99, 100, 101, 104, 105, 106, 107, 108, 111, 112, 113, 115, 116, 117, 118, 122, 123, 134, 135, 138, 144, 145, 146, 147, 148, 149, 150.

words, "Praise the Lord."* In the Hebrew, the word is *hallelujah*. Praise Yahweh. Praise the God of Abraham, Isaac, and Jacob. Praise the God of creation, covenant, and exodus. Praise the God of cross, resurrection, and new creation. Praise the Lord of hosts, the one enthroned on high. Praise the Lord, our refuge and strength.

The psalmists knew that the best place to begin in prayer is with God. It's not wrong to begin with pouring out our thoughts and feelings to God; dozens of psalms begin with lament, petition, thanksgiving, or other forms of prayer. Remember: if you're new to prayer or just "having a day," any prayer is better than no prayer. But as we mature in a praying life, we discover the wisdom of the Psalms in this pattern. If we begin with our problems and needs and forget who it is we're praying to, we may end up stuck in our problems and needs. To begin with God is to get ourselves in the best possible place to pour out our hearts.

When we see God for who he is, we can't help but be overwhelmed by his glory and praise him forever. Like the prophet Isaiah, who saw a heavenly vision of God high and lifted up, we look to God in prayer and praise and cry out, "My eyes have seen the King!" (Isa. 6:5). This is true spiritual experience. It's not an emptying of the mind or mere inspiration. A truly spiritual experience always includes beholding the living God as he truly is. And God is happy to provide us with a right view of him, calling us deeper into his praise. Why? Because he's always going after our hearts. This is why God revealed himself to Isaiah (and Moses and Joshua and Jeremiah and Ezekiel) personally. It's why Jesus called each of his disciples individually, by name. Because God is

---

* Psalms 103, 104, 106, 111, 112, 113, 117, 134, 135, 146, 147, 148, 149, 150.

not merely going after mere followers and servants. He wants our hearts. He wants us.

As I've said before, God doesn't need servants. He doesn't need a million little minions out here doing his will. "God longs to find in us a heart in love."[11] He's after our hearts. He longs for us to see him as he is and worship him, be overjoyed in his presence, eager to go where he goes and be where he is. This is what God longs for—for us to see him and not just know about him, but to truly know him. To delight in him, come alive in him, draw near to him. Jesus has made the way for us to draw near to God and see him as he is (and not be destroyed). Jesus was the sacrifice on that altar, so that our sin could be forgiven and our guilt removed.

As Keller has said, "The reason Jesus died on the cross was not so you could run programs and go to meetings. People can do all sorts of religious activity without Jesus's death and resurrection. He died so you can have access to God."[12] This is true Christianity, true spiritual experience: to draw near to the Father of glory and mercy through Jesus, and to say from the heart, "My eyes have seen the King!"

The best way to grow in adoration is to begin with Scripture. One of my regular prayer habits is to read the five "Psalms of the Day." (This method is described in Don Whitney's *Praying the Bible*.[13]) On the first day, you'll read Psalms 1, 31, 61, 91, and 121. You may read them each straight through fairly quickly, then pick one to meditate on. What is it saying? What does it tell you about who God is? Next, write out a few verses that you want to remember and consider throughout the day. After writing out these verses, turn them into a prayer of praise. It might look like this:

Scripture

> God is our refuge and strength,
> > an ever-present help in trouble.
>
> Therefore we will not fear, though the earth give way
> > and the mountains fall into the heart of the sea. (Ps. 46:1–2)

Prayer

Father God, you are my refuge and my strength.
You always help me in my time of need.
I'm afraid of so many things; I play out so many scenarios of trouble in my life.
But I can trust in you because you hold all things together.
Praise you, Lord God!
Everything else falls apart, but you remain the same forever.
You are my strength, O God!

Pretty simple, right? But do this every day for a month, and you'll cover all 150 Psalms. See how your view of God and life change. Imagine praying your praise every day for a year. What would it look like to build a life of daily adoration, year after year, decade after decade?

Praise the Lord. Behold him in all his glory. Let this vision of God (as he is) direct you in all you do. Let his power and unfailing love move you into Christlikeness. Pray your praise, and adore the God who made you, redeemed you, and loves you dearly.

Practice #2: Descending with the Mind into the Heart (Contemplation)

Contemplative prayer is conversation with God that is primarily marked by silence, listening, and meditating upon God's character and Word. Jesus told his disciples not to pray on street corners to be seen by others, but instead to go into their room and close the door. The "room" he was referring to was an inner room or closet in a house. Jesus was basically saying, "Go into your pantry, close the door, and pray." All private prayer thrives in safe, solitary places. But contemplative prayer is especially so. It's the unseen, go-into-your-closet-and-shut-the-door prayer. It's a second form of prayer designed to set our hearts at rest.

Some might be unfamiliar or even skeptical toward meditation and contemplation. They might say it sounds too "new agey." But rightly understood, contemplative prayer is *old* agey. It's as old as the Old Testament. The Scriptures are full of meditative, contemplative, heart-at-rest prayers. See, God's people have practiced meditation for several millennia (see: the Psalms). We were made to connect deeply with our Creator, attentive to our souls and his creation. The modern trends of daily reflection, yoga, and gratitude lists seek to fulfill this innate purpose. Many people meditate on the wrong things and in the wrong ways, but we were made to meditate.

Think about it: even non-Christians find themselves praying in times of crisis. I remember being on a Zoom call during the Covid pandemic with a group of creatives. I don't think the facilitator was a believer, but when she was trying to get the screen sharing to work (with fifty-some people waiting on mute), she could be heard muttering, "Please let this work, please let this work." Who was she talking to? She was instinctively talking to God. And not just praying, but repeating the same phrase over and over, the overflow of a heart made to meditate and ask for help in times of need.

Indeed, prayer is the most natural thing there is. We repeat those pleading *please* prayers in desperate times and trivial times alike—whether we're looking for a cancer cure or a parking spot. These internal dialogues and prayers show us that we were made for this. We are inherently pray-ers. And most of our prayers are contemplative in nature. We're reflecting on life and seeking divine presence and help.

Properly understood, then, this is true:

> We are built for contemplation. [It is the] subtlest, simplest, and most searching of the spiritual [practices]. Communion with God in the silence of the heart is a God-given capacity, like the rhododendron's capacity to flower, the fledgling's for flight, and the child's for self-forgetful abandon and joy.... God is our homeland. And the homing instinct of the human being is homed on God. As St. Augustine put it "we must fly to our beloved homeland. There the Father is, and there is everything."[14]

We were made to sit silently alone in God's presence (and therefore not alone at all). There we discover that if we can push through the distraction, the internal chatter, we will want to pray. We might find ourselves praying, "Heavenly Father. You are so good. Your name is great. Be glorified in all the world, Lord. Be honored in me, Lord. Be glorified in my life. Father, Hallowed be your name!"

Silence and solitude are critical to contemplative prayer. Solitude shows us how to let our hearts and minds be shaped by

God's presence more than the world's influences. Silence keeps us from getting suffocated in a world of words and noise and nonsense.

When we look at our lives, objectively from the outside, what do we see? We are a hurried people. We have many things to do, people to meet, texts and emails to respond to, events to attend, projects to complete, goals to reach. Often, I can get so hurried with activity that I don't stop to think, "Is this actually worth doing?"

Contemplative prayer helps to break us of all this external rubbish. Busyness and hurry and desire for okayness are not bad in themselves. But they typically reveal an inner disposition of self-trust and self-concern. If we can reorient ourselves to God and dwell pleasantly in the silence and solitude of his presence, we will find ourselves with a heart at rest.

Heart-at-rest prayer, Keller explains, may be marked by a sense of God's presence, assurance that we belong to God, an indescribable peace or joy, and soon, a transformed approach to life. This is the beauty of contemplative prayer: It's hard to describe because it's a wordless, happy sitting in the presence of God. It's a deep reflection into our own souls, asking God to reveal what's going on down there. And it's a deep, face-to-face sitting together with our Creator and heart's desire.

This contemplative type of prayer doesn't come naturally for many of us. I am, by nature, a more intellectually oriented, emotionally reserved person. I'm still not very aware of my inner world, despite the best efforts of Jessie and several spiritual directors. I'm more comfortable in rigorous Bible study than in heart-at-rest prayer. So the task of prayer for me, as an old contemplative writer put it, is "to descend with the mind into the heart."* True prayer doesn't

---

*This phrase has been attributed to many spiritual writers over the centuries, but it seems to originate with Saint Theophan the Recluse, an Eastern monk with one of the coolest names in all church history.

turn the mind off, but it goes much deeper. The mind and the heart become one, and we sit contentedly in the Father's presence.

We can't generate this kind of prayerful, praise-filled experience; it's a gift of God. And the experience itself is not the goal. The goal is intimacy with God, and experiences are wonderful gifts along the way. We don't focus on the gift but on the Giver. Yet when the gift is given, how sweet it is to sit in the presence of the Lord with a heart at rest!

But along the way, as we see God as he is and meditate on his greatness, we might also see ourselves in a new light. We might see quite a bit of unloveliness and ungodliness in our own hearts. What do we do with this?

Practice #3: Collapsing into Jesus (Confession)

It's always amazing to me how seamlessly the psalmists shift gears between forms of prayer as they pour out their hearts to God. One moment, they'll be praising God, then they'll burst into petition. They'll be asking for their needs, then lament the brokenness of the world around them. After a moment of lament, they'll suddenly begin confessing their sins. This is because prayer is relationship, not duty. It's the same way we connect with our best friends, spouses, parents, children, and coworkers. This is instructive as we witness the way the psalmists practice confession—the act of admitting specific sins, searching for unknown sins, and turning from all that is not glorifying to God.

On this side of the cross and resurrection, we have even more incentive to come to the Father with our sins in full view. We know Christ's work on the cross is finished and that it accomplished the forgiveness of our sins and direct access to God (Heb. 4:14–16).

We know Christ rose from the grave in victory over sin's power (Col. 2:13–15). We know that Christ now intercedes for us (Heb. 7:25); indeed, the Holy Spirit does as well (Rom. 8:26–27). What does all this mean? It means *we no longer have to hide*. We no longer have to minimize, explain away, debate, or refuse to see our ongoing sin. Jesus came to set the captives free, and that means us: we are no longer enslaved to sin. We can freely confess our sins before the Father and trust that our relationship to him is not weakened, it's strengthened. Indeed, our sins draw out the compassion of Jesus and the patience of the Father.[15] This is not incentive to sin; it's grace to honestly and quickly bring the fullness of our sin to our gracious triune God. We who truly love God will find ourselves rejecting sin out of a far greater motivation than rote obedience; we hate sin because we love him more.

Remember Jack Miller's wisdom from chapter three: maturing in Christ means repenting more quickly, not less often. Confession becomes a joy and a delight to the child of God living before the face of God. If we know the heart of God for us, though we may feel great shame over our sin against this holy and wonderful God, we will quickly return to him and seek his mercy—knowing full well he delights to forgive and renew us.

Psalm 73 is a great pattern for our confession prayers. Asaph, the great worship leader of Israel in the days of King David, wrote this:

> But as for me, my feet had almost slipped;
> I had nearly lost my foothold.
> For I envied the arrogant
> when I saw the prosperity of the wicked.
> (vv. 2–3)

Asaph is setting the theme for this prayer. He is saying, "I look around at my non-believing friends, and I became jealous and angry." He continues to say that as he looks at the lives of the wicked, they seem carefree, luxurious, and enviable. We can relate to this. We see our rude, hurried, self-centered peers getting ahead of us in life. They get more promotions, drive newer SUVs, live in larger homes, and send their kids to better schools. We grow resentful and begin to wonder if all this "following God" business is all it's cracked up to be.

In Psalm 73, Asaph goes on stewing over this for about a dozen verses. Finally, he laments, "Surely in vain I have kept my heart pure and washed my hands in innocence. All day long I have been afflicted, and every morning brings new punishments" (vv. 13–14). Okay, now he's being a little dramatic. *Every* morning brings new punishments? Probably not, but it's how he feels. It's an honest admission of frustration and confusion.

Then, finally, something changes. Something interrupts his complaining and self-pity. What happens? He enters the sanctuary of God (v. 17). In a moment, everything becomes clear. He can see the true state of these fools, and he can perceive their end—they will follow their own path all the way to eternal destruction and damnation (vv. 18–20). In this moment, he also sees himself in a new light. He recognizes his own sin. He admits that he's been "grieved and . . . embittered, I was senseless and ignorant; I was a brute beast before you" (vv. 21–22). What a great phrase! How often I have been a brute beast raging and bucking against a pure and steadfast God. But our Father endures our kicking and screaming and is still there when we lose our steam. And as he continues to patiently smile upon us, we look at all we have in Christ and realize *we* are the fools. We have everything. We have God himself.

And yet, we shake our fists at him and at the world. Finally, we can see our own sin and begin to confess and repent before him again.

In the end, Asaph is transformed. He's poured out his heart, in the presence of God, a prayer that's confession, lament, and praise all jumbled up. He is honest and direct, and—this is critically important for confession—*specific* and *tangible*. He is clear about his sin. Many Christians I've sat with over the years struggle with confession, even though they'll defend themselves and say that they're awful and confess their sin all the time. But just saying, "I'm the worst; I'm chief of sinners; I'm just generally quite bad" is not all that helpful. Sin is never general, and beating ourselves up for something generic doesn't make much sense. Sin is particular and specific. Importantly, it's personal. It's relational. All sin is against a personal God. (Most sin is against others as well, but first and foremost, it's against God.)

This is true confession, and it's a wonderful way to collapse on Jesus again. We rage and kick against God, and in the end, he's still there. Jesus is still interceding for us. And, like Asaph, everything has become clear again; we see our own sin with greater clarity than the sins of those around us. And we can only conclude, "Whom have I in heaven but you? And earth has nothing I desire besides you. My flesh and my heart may fail, but God is the strength of my heart and my portion forever" (vv. 25–26).

This is a beautiful pattern for our own prayers of confession. We begin with honesty and dump out our frustrations, and in the quiet, when we are faced with our own corrupt inner selves, we begin to see our sinfulness with clarity. We seamlessly transition into confession as the Lord reveals our sin. In other words, confession isn't just stating our known sins, it patiently waits to discover

Heart-at-Rest Prayer

sins not yet known, so that we can release those as well (see also Ps. 139:24).

For the child of God, this whole process is a joy. It's a treasure. We don't have to posture and blame and defend ourselves. In fact, we will only love God and others to the extent that we understand how forgiven we are (Luke 7:36–50). Surely our sin is more than we can bear, but we can pour out our hearts in the presence of this good and loving Father and fall again into Jesus.

Getting Our Souls in a Happy Place

When we regularly engage in these three forms of prayer—adoration, contemplation, and confession—we discover a powerful source of life and hope for daily life. We find within ourselves a heart at rest. When we do this daily, we have the potential to get our souls in a happy place.

In the nineteenth century, George Mueller devoted his life to serving the poorest and most disadvantaged children in Europe. He cared for more than ten thousand orphans and started eleven schools that provided education for more than 120,000 children. In his biography, he explains that he used to struggle with distraction in prayer. Then he made a discovery:

> I [now see] that the first great and primary business to which I ought to attend every day was to have my soul happy in the Lord. The first thing to be concerned about was not how much I might serve the Lord, how I might glorify the Lord; but how I might get my soul into a happy state, and how my inner man might be nourished.[16]

It is nearly impossible to get our souls happy in the Lord in a noisy environment. Of course, there's much more to the Christian life than the feeling of happiness. But I'm guessing you long for happiness as much as I do. Mueller's life was certainly busier than ours, as he traveled from country to country, starting orphanages and caring for children and staff. But he found a time and place to quiet his mind and feed his soul on the Word and presence of God.

As I write, I'm in the living room of our home. Our three boys are each at school, and my wife, Jessie, is working. It's a privilege to have the time and space for quiet reading, prayer, reflection, and writing. Earlier today, I was responding to emails and texts; later, I will be in meetings, having folks over for dinner, and putting the kids to bed. But right now, things are quiet. It's fall, and the wind is blowing with varying intensity. Our 1970s ranch house sits on a few acres and backs up to woods near Rock Bridge State Park. Large windows and sliding glass doors cover the rear of the house, so all we can see is a small forest of oak trees, with their green, yellow, and orange leaves rustling in the wind and blowing away toward the west. And it is quiet. (I'm thankful for my many friends who have chosen to start churches or take jobs in big cities, but for me, I'll take the quiet countryside of Central Missouri.)

And yet, even now, despite this picturesque venue and many years of praying in silence, I can't help but feel busy and anxious. I wonder if I should return to emails instead of working on this book. I feel like I'm behind on everything. I'm continually tempted to open my web browser and see if anything new has happened in the sports world. The silence is both therapeutic and maddening. I want to turn on music, shout, check my phone for new messages. My brain has been so shaped by noise and busyness, even quiet work is disorienting.

The good news, for me and for you, is that a heart at rest is possible. I have found this to be a wonderfully encouraging posture to take when I begin in prayer and reading God's Word. My goal is simply to get my soul into a happy place before God. To get there, I need a quiet, still environment (which often means getting up at 4:30 a.m., but more on prayer rhythms later). I typically open the Psalms and read three to five slowly and reflectively. And then I write out my prayers until I begin to feel the Father's presence surrounding me. Many times, I feel nothing. Often, my prayer time ends without a happy soul. But even more often, I limp into the silence and float out. I come weary, distracted, grumpy, and with a thousand burdens. But after pouring out my heart in silence, I get up with a fresh strength and peace, with a strange and resilient happiness.

It's ironic, isn't it? The place where we do our deepest, most important work in life—it's sitting quietly in a chair with the door closed. It's on our knees with our eyes closed. It's silence before an open Bible. Hands raised in worship, not busy in typing or building or working.

As Richard Foster once wrote, "the desperate need today is not for a greater number of intelligent people, or gifted people, but for deep people."[17] From solitude, we have something to offer in relationship. From silence, we have something to offer in our speech. Through prayer, we step out into the world with the heart and mind of Christ.

Good heavenly Father,
Here I confess my need of you again.
Quiet my environment and still my busy mind;
let me be at ease in your presence.
In you, I have every good thing.
Lead my heart into a happy place.
Let me grow more comfortable in silence,
show me my hidden sin,
and restore me in the goodness of your mercy and love.
Oh, how much I need your Son, the Lord Jesus!
Only in his name I pray, amen.

5

Heaven-on-Earth Prayer

In the Scriptures, God gives his people a surprising and uncomfortable amount of participation in his eternal purposes. As we have briefly said, he often waits to fulfill his plans until he can fulfill them through us. He waits till we pray. He is in no discernable hurry. He instead moves in our hearts to seek him, desire his kingdom on earth, and boldly ask for his glory to cover the earth. Our prayers literally do change the world. God has ordained this unexpected and strange pathway to his glory, and indeed, he is the one who gets the glory in the end.

In the last chapter, we discovered heart-at-rest prayer. In this chapter, we will explore what we might call "heaven on earth" prayer.

Most prayer books focus on one side of prayer or the other. They typically focus on intimacy or action. They emphasize either prayers that set our hearts at rest or prayers that call heaven to come to earth.* That's good and well, because we can happily read book after book on prayer and synthesize it all. But there's a dichotomy here that doesn't need to exist. We don't have to focus on either getting our hearts at rest or setting our world right. Prayer is a seamless means to both. If we are to follow the pattern of Jesus, the Psalms, and the apostles, we'll continually find ourselves doing both.

Think again of the Lord's Prayer, Jesus's pattern for our daily, moment-by-moment prayers. My belief is that you cannot pray the Lord's Prayer honestly without being drawn into the Lord's work.[1] You cannot pray "Hallowed be your name" without wanting to spread the name of the Lord far and wide. You cannot pray "Your kingdom come" without joyfully getting in on that kingdom life and mission. You cannot pray "deliver us from evil" without soon finding yourself working for the deliverance of others from the cruel and unjust schemes of evil in the world.

To pray the Lord's Prayer is a bold risk, and as we pray it—as it was meant to be prayed—nothing will quite be the same again. To quote N. T. Wright:

> When we call God "Father," we are called to step out, as apprentice children, into a world of pain and darkness. We will find that darkness all around us; it will terrify us, precisely because it will remind us of the darkness inside our own selves. The temptation then is to switch off the news, to shut out the pain of the world, to create a painless world for ourselves. A good deal of our

---

* There are several notable exceptions, such as E. M. Bounds's books, but it's hard to do in less than eight volumes.

contemporary culture is designed to do exactly that. No wonder people find it hard to pray.²

Yes and amen. When we pray, we are drawn into the heart of God. And as we are drawn into the heart of God, we are drawn into the work of God. He draws us in to send us out. He changes us to change the world. As it is said, hurt people hurt people. But this is also true: changed people change people. When we step out into the terrifying darkness all around us, keeping a lifeline to the Father in prayer, we find that we can and will make a notable difference in the world. But it's not so much by our actions as our prayers.

There are at least two forms of prayer that set our world right: intercession and petition. Praying for others and praying for our own wants and needs. We'll look at each in turn.

Practice #4: On Earth as in Heaven (Intercession)

The Pulitzer-nominated novelist Frederick Buechner used the word *bold* in writing about the Lord's Prayer. Have you thought of the boldness required to pray the Lord's Prayer truthfully? We are praying "Hallowed be your name"—above every other name, empire, corporation, and brand on earth. We are praying "Your kingdom come"—in direct attack on the kingdoms of our age. We are praying "Your will be done"—we are asking God to do *what he wants*, no matter what that brings.

And this phrase, most of all, demands boldness: "On earth as it is in heaven." How could Jesus teach us to pray this? Are we really ready for the implications of such a prayer? To pray this phrase is to lower ourselves to our earthiness and at once appeal for God's holy fire to fall on us. May earth look a little more like heaven. May our little world suddenly become more consumed with your presence, Father, Son, and Holy Spirit. To pray "on earth as it is in heaven" is borderline reckless, at least from an earthly point of view. Buechner writes:

> We do well not to pray the [Lord's Prayer] lightly. It takes guts to pray it at all. . . . "Thy will be done" is what we are saying. . . . And if that were to suddenly happen, what then? What would stand and what would fall? Who would be welcomed in and who would be thrown . . . out? . . . Boldness indeed. To speak those words is to invite the tiger out of the cage, to unleash a power that makes atomic power look like a warm breeze.³

When Jesus's friends asked him how to pray, his response offered a pattern for prayer that is both audacious and childlike, reckless and wise, all-encompassing and particular, transcendent and earthy. To pray the Lord's Prayer is an act of bold confidence in the power and graciousness of God. It is an invitation to life with God. It's a raw confession of need. It's a lament for the sick, poor, marginalized, and oppressed. It's a loud cry for mercy and justice. It's a vision for revival. It's a call to life together.

But most of all, it's a song of promise that will one day be fulfilled. One day, *it will be* on earth as it is in heaven. All shall be well. Injustice will be no more, chronic pain and infectious disease will be no more, every tear will be wiped away, and every wound will be healed by the Great Physician.

Intercession is the most dynamic and yet most overlooked form of prayer in today's church. More than just "praying for others," intercession compels God to *be who he is* in a particular place and time. We know that God is faithful; in intercession, we ask him to be faithful in a certain way to a particular person. We know that God is loving; in intercession, we ask him to reveal his love to our friend or coworker. Intercessory prayer begins with an acknowledgment of God's greatness and compassion, then calls on God to apply his character and power to someone who needs it most. In this way, we're seeking to compel our good Father to action, not by our own credibility but by *his*.

Here's what that can look like.

> Father, you have promised that your glory will cover the earth (Hab. 2:14); will you reveal yourself now in Columbia, Missouri? Glorify yourself in this particular time and city!

> Lord Jesus, you are the friend of sinners (Matt. 11:19); my friend Eric doesn't know you and is resistant to your good news; will you break through his stubborn heart and reveal your love to him?

> Lord, you are the God of healing (Ps. 103:3); will you heal my friend Jamie of her chronic illness? Let yourself be glorified by showing that you still heal the sick and brokenhearted today!

> Lord Jesus, there is much spiritual opposition against our church leaders right now, but you came to disarm all rulers and principalities of evil (Col. 2:15). Will you defend and protect us against the attacks of the enemy against us?

Father, you are just and merciful, a God who delights in justice, hates wrongdoing, and loves the stranger (Ps. 86:15; Isa. 61:8; Lev. 19:34); will you now defend the refugees in our city and overthrow the system of injustice that works against them?

Intercessory prayer is one of the means by which God moves history forward. In his infinite wisdom and patience, he often waits to fulfill his purposes until we pray. He could do everything without us, no doubt. But because he loves us and cherishes relationship with us, he often delays the fulfillment of his promises until we pray specifically and earnestly. He doesn't need us, but he *wants* us to be involved.

Take the example of Moses. We know Moses as the great leader of Israel, and we know him as one of the Old Testament's preeminent prophets too. But have we considered the remarkable prayer life of Moses? God would often draw Moses to himself for days at a time, revealing himself and his will to Moses. In Exodus 32, the Israelites get tired of waiting for Moses to come down from the mountain, and they quickly spiral into corruption and make a golden calf out of their gold jewelry. Moses is distraught over their sin, and knowing God to be holy and righteous, fears that Israel might be completely wiped out. Moses goes directly to the Lord in prayer and asks that God forgive their sin (v. 32). God responds that he will punish them for their sin but agrees not to totally destroy his people (vv. 33–35).

God tells Moses he will still give the Israelites the Promised Land, but he will not personally lead them anymore—the pillar of cloud, representing his presence, would not remain with them. He will instead send an angel to go before them (33:1–3). So,

Heaven-on-Earth Prayer

Moses's first prayer has been granted, but he's not done yet. Moses approaches God a second time in the tent of meeting. It's here that we learn that God would regularly speak to Moses face-to-face, as one talks with a friend (33:11). In this prayer conversation, Moses makes his second request, citing God's own character and goodness first. He prays, "Remember that this nation is your people" (33:13). He's appealing to God's own faithfulness and steadfast love. Moses continues, "If your Presence does not go with us, do not send us up from here" (33:15). He's saying: If you don't personally come with us, God, what is the point of any of it? It's not enough to send an angel. We want *you*, God!

Now, this is a bold second request, and we might fear that God will respond with anger. We might tell Moses he should be content with his first request being answered. But one answered prayer has a way of increasing our faith and boldness. So Moses makes this second request, and it seems to delight God even more. God responds, "I will do the very thing you have asked, because I am pleased with you and I know you by name" (33:17). Prayer number two is also answered.

Now, I played basketball every day through high school and college, and I can tell you this. If I made a three-pointer, it made me want to shoot another three. And if I made two threes? You couldn't stop me from taking a third. I tell my boys the same thing: if you're hot, it's no time for meekness; keep shooting! I think Moses is thinking essentially the same thing now. He's two for two. In the language of NBA Jam, he's heating up. Why not go for three?

With a preposterous boldness, Moses makes a third request, and it's the most audacious one yet. "Now show me your glory" (33:18). Can you believe it? Moses asks to *see* God in all his glory. But no one can see God and live (33:20)! Has Moses lost his mind?

Or is he perhaps as close to the heart of God as he's ever been? Is he actually asking God for the exact sort of thing that God wants to give? Indeed, God's response tells us everything. He will do it. He will allow his goodness to pass in front of Moses, but God will not show his face—because Moses would not survive that one (33:19–23). The following day, Moses prepares himself and returns up the mountain. It says that "the Lord came down in the cloud and stood there with him. . . . And he passed in front of Moses," proclaiming his name (34:5–6). All because Moses dared to ask.

Boldness, indeed. Moses has moved from intercession to petition with this third request, but he's not shifting gears too much. He is asking God to be who he is in some particular way. Moses is bringing God's own character and goodness before him, seeking more of his presence and power. He's asking God to do the very thing that he wants to do. And God delights to answer each and every request.

Intercessory prayer becomes our joy as we experience the thrill of answered prayer. Reading the stories of Moses—not to mention the accounts of Elijah and others—it seems clear that we are not asking God for too much, but too little. People often say that the most difficult thing about prayer is unanswered prayer. I'm not sure about that. I wonder if the most disorienting thing is *answered* prayer. When God actually answers out prayers specifically and powerfully, it blows us away. We experience a holy fear of God, like the disciples in the boat when Jesus calmed the wind and waves— they suddenly became more afraid in the presence of Jesus than they were over the storm (Mark 4:41). There's just no going back to "normal" once you see the hand of the Lord working right in front of you.

If we're not asking for much in prayer, we don't get much from God. Jesus said, "Ask and you shall receive." James added, "You don't have because you don't ask." Perhaps we're afraid God won't answer. Or perhaps we're more afraid he *will* answer! In intercessory prayer, we're asking God to change the world. We're asking him to make it a more just, more God-aware, more beautiful place. We're asking him to change our friends' hearts and lives. We're seeking his justice to roll like a river. We're asking him to *be who he is* in some particular way. And God delights in these prayers! But it's not the only type of prayer that changes the world, nor the only kind that sparks God's delight.

Practice #5: The Most Basic and Important of Prayers (Petition)

Petition, also called supplication, is the form of prayer we are most familiar with, and it holds a secure place in the life of the growing believer. Since we are needy people, we can bring all our needs before the Father with boldness and humility. Prayer is largely just asking for what we want and need.

Petition is probably the most natural form of prayer. It's when we lift our voice or thoughts instinctively to God and say, "Help." Petition will likely be the dominant form of prayer in our own prayer lives. However, when we see petition in the Psalms, it's different in some important ways from our most natural prayers. But before we get into the Psalms, let's remember why we have such a hard time asking in the first place.

Why We Struggle to Ask

Think back to the comedian's joke about prayer that I mentioned in the introduction. The fact that Gervais could openly make fun of believers for praying earnestly shows us the dominant view of our day. If you live in America or another Western country, you likely experience this every day. I live in a highly progressive college town, and I know it represents the typical mindset of my neighbors as well.

In brief, we struggle to ask God for much because we've been shaped by our secular age's rejection of the supernatural. Our culture might not persecute us for our faith, but we certainly won't be praised for relying on God more than ourselves. We've been surrounded by this assumption that we are responsible for making things happen, and that everything relies on our success or failure. If there is a God, our neighbors likely believe, he's not actively involved in daily life. To put our faith, hope, and trust in an unseen God is considered wishful thinking at best, and at worst, total lunacy.

So we are swimming upstream to even pray at all. It takes an incredibly bold act of foolishness (in the best sense) to pray for help, for strength, for guidance, for forgiveness of sin, for healing for someone else, for renewal in our lives. It's far easier to say, "God, I don't know if you want to answer my prayers, so just increase my faith and contentment, and I'll see you when I get to heaven." It's much more difficult to pray, "Father, if you don't show up right now, this whole thing's gonna fall apart."

The good news is we *can* be transformed by the renewing of our minds. We have to immerse ourselves more in the Scriptures than ever before, asking God to give us his own heart and mind toward prayer.

Why We Can Ask

I have found Psalm 86 to be a great pattern for our prayers of petition. It's the only psalm of David in book three of the Psalms, and it gives us a glimpse into the king's boldness in asking for his wants and needs. He begins with a combination of adoration and petition.

> Hear me, LORD, and answer me,
> for I am poor and needy. . . .
> You are my God; have mercy on me, Lord,
> for I call to you all day long. . . .
> Hear my prayer, LORD;
> listen to my cry for mercy.
> When I am in distress, I call to you,
> because you answer me. (vv. 1–7)

That last line is one of my favorites: "I call to you, because you answer me." It's simple and profound at the same time. We can ask God for what we want and need, because God does answer us. And even more, we have his character we can look upon. That's what David does. He says, "You, Lord, are forgiving and good, abounding in love to all who call to you" (v. 5). He continues on, "Among the gods there is none like you, Lord; no deeds can compare with yours. . . . For you are great and do marvelous deeds; you alone are God" (vv. 8, 10). Like Moses, he is coming before God declaring God's character and faithfulness. David is not appealing to his own righteousness (except maybe a bit in verse 2), but he's calling to mind God's infinite power and mercy as he asks for what he wants and needs.

What a perfect pattern for our own asking. "I call to you, because you answer me." Our Father is the God who hears and answers prayer. For centuries, he has been hearing the voices of his children as they seek him. For generations, he has delighted to answer prayers and bless his people with his presence.

What to Ask For

Next, notice that David asks four main things of the Lord—*protection, inner devotion, strength*, and *joy*.

He asks for *protection*. "Guard my life . . . have mercy on me. . . . Arrogant foes are attacking me, O God. . . . Save me" (Ps. 86:2–3, 14, 16). The number one issue facing David right now is a big one. His enemies are attacking him and trying to kill him. David starts with his biggest, most urgent need—protection. In our own prayers, we can and should start with our most pressing needs. Even if it seems too obvious to pray for, even if you prayed about it yesterday and the day before and the day before, ask and ask again and keep on asking.

He asks for *inner devotion*. "Teach me your way, Lord . . . give me an undivided heart" (v. 11). The climax of the passage is David's appeal for an undivided heart. An undivided heart means we are wholly devoted to God. An undivided heart protects us from asking for the wrong things. This may seem like an odd petition, since David is in dire straits, with enemies seeking to kill him. But he knows how easily he can become divided in his devotion and distracted in his pursuits. Even amid great stress, he asks for something God surely wants to give him. In the same way, we would do well to include in all our petitions a request for increased devotion, single-minded faith, and an undivided heart.

He asks for *strength*. "Turn to me and be gracious to me; give your strength to your servant" (v. 16 ESV). Some translations will say "show your strength," but the original emphasis is on God giving his strength to David in a time of need. The king knows he won't be able to get through the day without God's strength. He is refusing to live in his own energy and ingenuity. God is infinite in his power, so why not ask him to give some of his strength to us?

Last, he asks for *joy*. "Bring joy to your servant, Lord, for I put my trust in you" (v. 4). How often do you ask for joy? Joy is one of the fruits of the Spirit (Gal. 5:22). Jesus said he came to make our joy complete (John 15:11). So clearly, joy is one of the marks of Christlikeness and a gift that God wants to regularly give us. Joy is deeper than the feeling of happiness. In the Bible, joy is the place of glad flourishing in the presence of God, where all of life is aligned and challenges are faced with God's presence.

At the end of Psalm 86, we see that even though David's circumstances haven't changed, he says in his final words, "you, Lord, have helped me and comforted me" (v. 17). Did you catch this? David opens his prayer by asking for help (v. 1: "Hear me, Lord, and answer me") and closes it by thanking God that he has received help. Before David is even done praying, God has already answered him. The Father is already giving him protection, devotion, strength, and joy.

This, perhaps, is a type of secret in prayer. We ask for what we want and need, and God gives us what we want and need—in his timing. But he also gives us even more than we ask for. He also gives us help, comfort, relationship, strength, guidance, wisdom, protection, and joy. We go in asking for a slice of bread and we come out with three loaves.

Of course, you can spend your time asking for all sorts of worldly blessings—a promotion at work, a perfectly-curated home, an off-the-grid vacation spot whose pictures will rock social media, or (for me) a high-end road bike—but this life is short and fleeting. The smart choice is seeking blessings that last into eternity—protection from the enemy, strength for our calling, singlemindedness for tough decisions, and joy in any kind of circumstance.

In all this asking in the Father's presence, we get our souls in a happy place *and* he answers our prayers. This business of asking may come naturally to us, and yet to grow in our boldness, expectation, and contentment, we would do well not to be alone in all of our asking.

Praying with One Another

Two days ago, I was sitting with a member in our church, a warmhearted man in his mid-sixties. In almost an offhand comment at the end, he told me of how his prayer life had changed in the last few years. He has been part of a friend group for more than two decades, a sweet and rare community that had helped each other raise kids and support one another through countless parties and tragedies. He said for all those years, they always shared everything with each other and promised to pray for each other. But he admitted it was so hard to remember to actually pray for them. These days however, after the entire group had joined our congregation, he said something has shifted. They still share everything with each other, but now they actually stop and pray together. If someone shares a struggle with another person, immediately they stop—whether in a living room, on a walk, or at Home Depot—and pray for each other. "It's remarkable," he told me. Absolutely it is. Praying *for* one another is a beautiful thing. But praying *with* one another is altogether heavenly.

In fact, the best way to pray *for* others is to pray *with* others. While this is a habit that can be cultivated in many ways, we've found that creating spaces where people pray with each other is essential. We make times in each of our community group meetings to pray together. Again, to not just share requests and pray later but actually pray together.

Further, I'm convinced that developing a praying life *at all* requires time spent praying with others—especially with those more comfortable in intercession and petition. The church has a secret weapon, yet it's often neglected. What is it? The prayer meeting. Prayer meetings have fallen on hard times. Almost every church I know offers some type of prayer meeting, and it's typically once per month and sparsely attended. But those who attend know the secret. They gather, undeterred by the low attendance. And they pray together, strengthening one another as they intercede for the church and pray for each other. Oh, what a glorious and life-changing time this can be! Oh, that our modern church would bring back this sacred time before the Lord.

Charles Spurgeon was a constant champion of the humble prayer meeting. When asked the secret of his power in preaching, he replied, "the boiler room." In each gathering, a small group of prayer warriors gathered in the basement boiler room beneath his pulpit. While he preached, they prayed. This work below, he knew, was just as essential and powerful as his work above. The faith in the basement spurred the faith above ground. Not only that, but Spurgeon preached over and over on prayer, and often spoke of the critical place of the prayer meeting in the life of the church.[4]

He may be remembered as the Prince of Preachers, but he knew this: his preaching gained its power from the prayers of many. And the way to learn prayer was not merely to teach on it, but to do it.

To gather together and pray and pray and pray. So it is today. Prayer is a team sport. We each have a role to play and we practice alone as well. But the real power in intercession and petition comes when we get in the same room, circle the chairs or get on our knees, and pour out our hearts together.

Praying for the Lost

When we discover Jesus's bold teachings on asking and receiving and we begin to pray "your kingdom come on earth as it is in heaven," we'll soon find ourselves praying for our lost friends, family members, neighbors, and coworkers. And prayer is "powerful and effective" (James 5:16) in multiple ways when we're interceding for the lost.

***Prayer gives us the heart of God** for the lost.*

It's impossible to draw near to the heart of God without also gaining his heart for the lost. You might bristle at the word *lost*. It seems insensitive and even arrogant to declare others lost. But this word actually comes from the way Jesus tells us God thinks of those outside his kingdom. In Luke 15, Jesus tells us three lost-and-found parables to describe the heart of God for those far from him. A shepherd loses one of his sheep and leaves the ninety-nine to find it (vv. 3–7). A woman loses a single coin and turns her home upside down till she finds it (vv. 8–10). A father loses his son to self-centered, licentious living in a distant land, but he gains him back when the prodigal finally returns home (vv. 11–32). In all three stories, Jesus tells us that the Father figure celebrates wildly when his lost treasure is restored. Our God is the Father who waits patiently, seeks diligently, and leaves his other duties (so to speak) to see his lost children come home.

***Prayer, practiced regularly, keeps us focused* on loving our lost friends.**

I have a short list of people I most want to see come to faith in Christ. The list includes a few family members, neighbors, and cycling buddies; I keep their names on a small sticky note inside my Bible. I've been praying for years, even decades, for some of them. It can be easy to lose energy in praying for these folks, especially when no effect is immediate and visible. But praying for them continually keeps them on our minds, so that when we see them next, we're prepared to ask thoughtful questions, make meaningful conversation, and persuasively communicate the good news.

Prayer takes the pressure off us in evangelism.

Jesus told his disciples to wait for the Holy Spirit before they started their new ministries (Luke 24:49). They were not to try to do this immensely difficult new work in their own strength; they were to wait for the Spirit. Notice the pattern in Acts: While waiting, they prayed (Acts 1:14, 24; 2:1). While praying, the Spirit came (2:2–4). When the Spirit came, they immediately began proclaiming the gospel (2:14–36). When they spoke the gospel, people were saved and baptized (2:41). And when people were baptized, they immediately began praying for others (2:42–47). Prayer is an essential part of the process of evangelism and conversion. It's one aspect of our work, but ultimately, it is the mission of Jesus to gather his lost sheep (John 10:16) and make them one with him in his kingdom (John 17:20–26). It is the Holy Spirit who convicts of sin (John 16:8–11) and brings about spiritual change (John 3:5–8). The pressure is off us; we need only pray and speak the word of the gospel.

Prayer has real power in drawing the lost toward God.

Not only does prayer prepare us to share the good news of Jesus with our lost friends, it also begins the process of fulfilling God's promises. Jack Miller writes,

> *Prayer starts the promises of God on their way to fulfillment.* Here is God's battle plan for our time. In prayer, God allows us to lay hold of His purposes as these are expressed in His promises. . . . By claiming God's promises as we petition Him in prayer, we set God's work in motion (Luke 10:1–3; Acts 4:23–31). Unbelievable as it may seem, the omnipotent God uses our requests to activate the fulfillment of His mighty promises in history (Rev. 8:1–5).[5]

Indeed, praying for our lost friends has immeasurable impact on our hearts, our friends, and our world. In our church, we pray together for our lost friends so regularly that we can name each other's non-believing friends—even when we haven't met them. I know who my closest friends are praying to see saved, because we've prayed for them together. And so you can imagine our shared joy when one of us has a meaningful spiritual conversation with someone we've been praying for together. And you can possibly even imagine the widespread celebration when one of these far-off friends becomes a follower of Jesus and is baptized in front of us. I suppose it's a final work of prayer in reaching the lost: *Prayer increases our joy when someone comes to faith in Jesus.*

When All Else Fails, Find Jesus and Fall at His Feet

As we close this chapter, think back to the story of Jesus's double healing. First, the synagogue leader came to Jesus with an intercessory prayer—"Heal my daughter." He was terrified at the thought of losing his daughter. He was desperate. This was no time for meekness. He found Jesus, cared nothing of what his fellow religious leaders would think, and fell at his feet. This is intercession. It's finding Jesus in our time of need and collapsing at his feet for the sake of another.

In the very same moment, here comes a woman with a chronic bleeding disorder. Hers was a prayer of petition—"Heal me." She was sick of her suffering, tired of visiting every doctor and trying every well-meaning friend's supplement recommendation. She was desperate. Would she ever get so close to Jesus again? With this whole crowd, she probably couldn't even get his attention. Again, no time for meekness. She pressed her way toward Jesus, cared nothing of what the others would think, and took the edge of his robe in her hand for only a moment. This is petition. It's finding Jesus in our time of need and collapsing at his feet.

If we were orphan kids, we would need to think carefully about our behavior. If we were servants, hoping to gain the favor of our manager, it would behoove us to consider the reasonableness of our requests. But as I've repeatedly said (and I've repeated it on purpose), *we're not orphans and we're not merely servants.* We're beloved children. Our Father stands ready to hear us. The Son has already pulled back the curtain. The Spirit is already interceding. Our God has taken all the initiative and is now waiting—waiting!—for us to turn to him. Will you do it? Will you find your Lord and fall at his feet? See his face, turning to you and smiling. Again, he asks you simply, "What is it you want?"

This, my friends, is prayer. Pour out your heart. If he doesn't answer yet, keep asking. Thank him for his presence anyway. If he answers your prayer, ask another one. If you're two for two, take a step back and let it fly again. What do you have to lose? Find Jesus and fall at his feet.

Father, all-powerful, good and loving:
This world is a broken, dangerous, and terrifying place.
We need you to be who you are.
Change the world, O God!
Bring your kingdom to earth! Make it down here like it is up there!
Do away with injustice, chronic pain, anxiety, cancer, and death once and for all.
In Columbia, Missouri, as it is in heaven.
In London, Nairobi, Tokyo, and Moscow, as it is in heaven.
In the city, in the country, in the home, and in my heart—as it is in heaven.
Come, Lord. Come! Amen.

6

Praying through Heartache

A certain type of ministry of the gospel is *cruel*. It doesn't mean to be, but it is."[1] I remember where I was when I read these words by the late theologian J. I. Packer. It was a season of great pain and heartache for me, and it's not an overstatement to say that Packer's words changed my life as I continued to read. What is the cruel sort of ministry that Packer had in mind? His answer has come to haunt me.

I was going through a particularly hard season of depression and had been suffering from chronic illness symptoms. It was a season of trial and discouragement that had lasted far too long, or so I thought. I had prayed. I had talked with wise counselors. I had prayed more. But this difficult season was unrelenting, and my spirit was not lifting.

It was at that time that my friend Kevin pointed me to Packer's *Knowing God*. I had read it before, but he pointed me back to a chapter late in the book called "These Inward Trials." That evening,

I reopened the classic book, found the chapter, and began to read. (Some lessons just can't be learned until we're ready.)

Packer's reflections helped me make sense of my season of hardship, and I wonder how many of us feel similarly burdened by our own unexpectedly long and demanding seasons. And I also wonder how many of us have unwittingly absorbed the teachings of this cruel gospel ministry. If we can understand, however, what Packer was getting at, if we can understand not only the cruel teaching but also the wonderful antidote, I am sure that we might find some hope in our inward trials.

These Inward Trials

So, what is this *cruel* sort of gospel ministry? According to Packer, the cruel teaching is that becoming a Christian makes your life easier. It's the idea that being a believer decreases your sinning, enables you to find your truest self and deepest calling, equips you to change the world, and means less overall suffering. In other words, we could summarize this cruel and unbiblical teaching as: Your Best Life Now!

The lopsided impression "which pictures the normal Christian life as trouble-free," Packer writes, "is bound to lead sooner or later to bitter disillusionment."[2]

If there's a phrase that encapsulates the spiritual condition of twenty and thirty-somethings that I've ministered among for the past decade-and-a-half, it's "bitter disillusionment." In the words of *Fight Club*'s Tyler Durden, "We've all been raised on television to believe that one day we'd all be millionaires, and movie gods, and rock stars. But we won't. And we're slowly learning that fact. And we're very, very [ticked] off."[3] Truly, we have been told we can change the world by our best efforts. And then we become adults and discover that life is pretty hard, we are not all that special, and this world is an ugly, vicious place.

Dietrich Bonhoeffer called this the "wish-dream." Why this phrase? He wrote *Life Together* in German, and apparently when his English translators came across this concept in his writing, they faced a lack of a better word, and so they came up with this one.[4] Although newer translations of *Life Together* use other words, the phrase "wish-dream" perfectly encapsulates his thinking. The wish-dream is the ideal of life as we think it should be, a life of happiness and meaning and satisfaction. It's a life without pain, without setbacks, without conflict, without suffering. Said another way, it's the picture-perfect image we have in our heads about the way our life was supposed to go before this fallen world got ahold of it.

We lay this wish-dream of the Christian life on others, unable to understand why they are struggling in their spiritual lives. When we do face hardship, we are shocked—we seek to blame others, make demands of God, or "spin" why it's not so bad. A failed wish-dream is the breeding ground for self-pity. As a result, our Christian communities can be broken down by the wish-dream, as we become disillusioned when it doesn't come true in our friendships and church growth.

"But God's grace speedily shatters such dreams," Bonhoeffer said, in order that he might rebuild us around reality.[5] In his grace (and it is sheer grace), God enables us to embrace the way of Jesus in a broken world.

Indeed, it is cruel ministry to call believers back to their wish-dream and suggest that Jesus and the church will make it all possible after all. Christ does change everything, but it's certainly not that simple. Packer continues:

> God doesn't make our circumstances notably easier [when we become Christians]; rather the reverse. Dissatisfaction recurs over wife, or husband, or parents, or in-laws, or children, or colleagues or neighbors. Temptations and bad habits which their conversion experience seemed to have banished for good reappear.[6]

Thankfully, the Scriptures don't leave us on our own when it comes to facing suffering. Ecclesiastes, the Old Testament book that crucifies the wish-dream, says: "[God] has set eternity in the human heart; yet no one can fathom what God has done from beginning to end" (3:11). Deep within us, a good and perfect life exists; yet we can't understand what God is doing in actual history.

As Tim Keller has shown in *Walking with God through Pain and Suffering*, suffering is one of the main themes of the Bible itself.[7] Genesis begins with an account of how evil and death came into the world. Exodus describes Israel's oppression in Egypt and their forty years in the wilderness, a time of trial and testing. The Psalms provide prayers for every situation in life, but the most frequent prayers are for help in need and comfort in suffering; its honest prayers describe the brutality of life and the injustice of suffering. Three Old Testament books—Job, Lamentations, and Ecclesiastes—have suffering as their main theme. Two New Testament books—Hebrews and 1 Peter—are focused on helping Christians face suffering, sorrows, and troubles. Most of all, the central Person of the Scriptures,

Jesus Christ, is called the Man of Sorrows (Isa. 53:3 ESV). "The Bible, therefore, is about suffering as much as it is about anything."[8]

Suffering is a significant theme on the pages of Scripture, and when we take all the pages together, we find a comprehensive view of pain and hardship. Where we want to find the easy, smooth road throughout the Bible, with maybe a couple quick platitudes we can use to comfort each other at funerals thrown in for good measure, we discover the hard road instead, full of threats and thickets and thorns. The Bible certainly gives a happy ending at the end of the grand story. But if you look at the lives and stories that make up this epic narrative of the Bible, you'll find that most of those stories don't give us only happy endings—at least not by the world's definition. Most chunks of the Bible are not a 22-minute TV episode with a full resolution before the end credits.

On the surface, that seems quite discouraging. But on the other hand, it's freeing and refreshingly *honest*. Isn't it wonderful to know that the Bible doesn't offer us meaningless platitudes that eventually fail us? Instead, it tells the truth that we are living in a broken world. It helps us face reality instead of deny it. And it helps us remember God hasn't promised freedom from suffering in this life. After all, it's important to know what God has promised and what he hasn't.

Keller uses the fiery furnace of Daniel 3 as an illustration for understanding how God uses suffering in our lives. Fire, of course, is a dangerous thing; it can be all-consuming, it can burn down a building, it can clear out an entire forest, and it can kill a person within moments. But fire, when used in a controlled and wise way, is one of the great gifts of life. Fire can be used to warm a home in the winter, refine a piece of metal, shape clay; it can be used to cook food. Without fire, there would be no barbecue! Fire, used rightly, doesn't burn; it shapes, refines, prepares, purifies, and beautifies. Fire *matures* things.

Suffering, in the same way, is absolutely painful, it feels like death; we can hardly bear it. And yet if faced with faith and endured in the presence of God, suffering shapes us, refines us, prepares us, purifies us, beautifies us. Suffering matures people. In the gospel, suffering takes evil and pain and turns it back on itself; through suffering we overcome evil and pain. Out of darkness comes light, and out of death comes new life.

What is the purpose of these trials? Packer gives us an illustration, which I'll summarize this way: A good father doesn't let his children go their own way. Even when it's costly, he leads them with mercy and wisdom. He allows the children to experience some of the world's pain yet remains with them through it all. This is God's grace to us. Through suffering in a broken world (broken by us, not by God), he builds our character, strengthens our faith, and prepares us to serve and help others. His strength is revealed in our weakness. Packer writes:

> How does God in grace [accomplish] this purpose [of maturing us]? Not by shielding us from assault by the world, the flesh and the devil, nor by protecting us from burdensome and frustrating circumstances . . . but rather by exposing us to all these things, so as to overwhelm us with a sense of our own inadequacy, and to drive us to cling to him more closely. . . . The reason why the Bible spends so much of its time reiterating that God is a strong rock, a firm defense, and a sure refuge and help for the weak is to bring home to us that

we are weak . . . [and must learn] "to wait on the Lord."[9]

This has been my experience. Other than perhaps daily time with the Lord in reading and prayer, nothing has changed me more than suffering. Nothing has brought me to the end of myself, and rooted out self-confidence, like suffering. Or as one of my mentors says: "Everybody grows by prayer or by pain . . . And no one gets there by prayer."[10]

Do I think God forces us to suffer only that we would learn hard lessons—like a cosmic PE coach? No. This world is cruel; God is good. But he certainly allows us to live in this broken world without shielding us from its pains and afflictions. And he certainly wants us to reckon with reality instead of wasting our days in a wish-dream. "In this world you will have trouble," Jesus said (John 16:33). Jesus doesn't ask the Father to protect us from all suffering, only that we are protected from the evil one (John 17:15). Through a hard life in a broken world, the Father has become more real to us in our tears and pain than in our laughter and peace. It's by suffering that we learn patience, endurance, trust, and hope. These are precious virtues that are impossible to shape without fire. If we want them, we must come to terms with the fact that they can only be forged in real life in the real world, not in a dream.

Practice #6: Praying through Heartache (Lament)

Now, back to prayer. What is the most important time to pray? While it's always a good time to pray, the most important time for prayer is the moment when we are most afraid, discouraged, hurt, and downcast. Said another way, the best time to pray is when we *least* feel like praying.

Lament is an essential form of prayer for life in a broken, crumbling world. Lament is the groaning of the broken heart, begging God for help, for mercy, for justice. Lament is the cry that God might intervene and set things straight. Lament is our way of praying, "Help God! Where are you? How long must this last?"

Maybe you were taught growing up not to talk back to God—not to yell at him, not to argue with him. The Psalms say: "Nope, you actually *should* pray this way. It's a primary form of prayer!" In fact, it's our sixth way to pour out your heart before God. The psalmists were masters of lament; it is the most consistent form of prayer in the Old Testament's prayer book.

Dozens of psalms instruct us in prayers of lament. Let's consider one of the simplest, cleanest laments: Psalm 13. King David, master of lament, opens his prayer like this:

> How long, Lord? Will you forget me forever?
> How long will you hide your face from me?
> How long must I wrestle with my thoughts
> and day after day have sorrow in my heart?
> How long will my enemy triumph over me?

What was leading David into this dark, prayerful place? He describes his condition. First, *he has sorrow in his heart, day after day.* He's downcast, disheartened, mourning. We're not sure why exactly. But his heart is broken. He's discouraged. He feels awful. He wants to feel better, but nothing helps.

Second, *he is wrestling with his thoughts.* Do you ever have this experience? You want your mind to relax but it keeps going back to your greatest fears and worst nightmares? Or you're in a really hard situation and it just keeps playing in your mind, like a movie that won't turn off? Or you're in conflict, and you keep having imaginary conversations with the other person? Day after day, wrestling, struggling.

Third, *David feels forgotten and abandoned by God.* He's asking: "Will you forget me forever? How long will you hide your face from me?" He looks around for God, and nothing happens. He goes to pray but feels nothing. He opens God's Word but nothing connects. He wants to be near God, but he can't feel God's presence at all. It seems God has forgotten him, or he's busy elsewhere. It's his time of great need, and God is nowhere to be found.

Fourth, *David feels rejected and scorned by others.* He's asking: "How long will my enemy triumph over me?" I'm not sure who this enemy is, probably not the enemies of Israel, but rather probably people within the nation that oppose him. His friends or family members or coworkers—they have rejected him; they have spoken against him; and then worst of all, they seem to be right. David seems to be defeated.

Maybe you resonate with one or two of these—if not all four. In our modern world, David would likely be diagnosed with depression, anxiety, loneliness, and maybe post-traumatic disorder at this low point in his life. In short, his life is falling apart. He's not just struggling—he's deeply, profoundly suffering. He references life and death, as if to say, "maybe death wouldn't be much worse than this." He's languishing, he's angry, and yet, get this: *he's bringing it all to God.*

Now, think about our own experience and culture for a moment. Mark Sayers observes that in American society especially, our foundation is the freedom of the individual.[11] Personal autonomy is our highest value; radical individualism shapes our lives.

Our culture demands, "No one can tell me who I am; no one can push their thoughts on me; I am me and I am free!"

The problem is that living isolated lives (even if you're married and in community, you can still be isolated by this framework of radical individualism) fills us with anxiety. The system itself is anxious; there's no stability, no accepted laws, no one to trust except however you happen to feel that day. Everything's a gray area. And that creates massive stress on our nervous systems. Think about it: if we have to figure it all out for ourselves, that's utterly exhausting.

The grand goal of our anxious society, then, is essentially comfort. Our persistent desire is to be successful outwardly and at peace inwardly. Sayers writes,

> In the contemporary world, feeling good is the expected normative state of being. When one doesn't experience good feelings—if a task is unpleasant, if a relationship goes through a difficult period, if a job is tough—it is taken as a signal that something is wrong, or that something is wrong with you.[12]

And we have so many anxious people and the whole system has anxiety baked into it—so now we have organizations and social groups that form comfort zones to protect us from the world without challenging us or asking us to grow or change into something more. So we're utterly anxious and uncomfortable, while everything around us is saying, "maybe if you just add this technique or product, then you'll be fine again." Basically, American culture does nothing to prepare us for suffering; instead, it tells us that if we're struggling, it's our fault too. And of course, I'm not pointing the finger at you if you struggle with depression and anxiety.

Not at all. Instead, I want to point at radical, anxious individualism that expects to experience nothing but comfort and enjoyment every moment of every day, and say, "*That* is why you struggle with depression and anxiety!" How could you not?

Think of it even more broadly. When we look around our world, we see pervasive injustice in our communities, persistent brokenness in our social systems. We live in a world of school shootings, systemic racism, local homelessness, global poverty, sex trafficking, child abuse, natural disasters, and a thousand other tragedies. Our pains are both personal and inward, *and* they're systemic and global.

Biblical lament is a believer's secret weapon in a hard, secular world. If we can learn to lament well, we'll find ourselves able to face each day's demands, trials, and afflictions with a prayerful spirit. Too often, we try to make our way *around* suffering. We are told to look for a silver lining or to think of others that have it much worse than us. But this is a mere minimizing of our suffering; there's no relief here. Lament is a way for us to fully acknowledge the hardship of our condition, and to, like David, take it all to God in prayer. The purpose of lament is to bring our sorrows, anxiousness, frustrations, and troubles to God.

Still, maybe, it feels wrong to unload our anger on God. J. I. Packer simply calls lament "complaining." He says complaining is one of the most important forms of prayer. If you're anything like me, you wonder how this could be allowed—after all, didn't the Israelites in the Old Testament get scolded for grumbling? Here's where it gets good. A prayer of lament is not complaining *about* God but *to* God.

The closer we are to our Father, the freer we'll feel to complain in his presence. Think of two children. The first is afraid of his father. He believes Dad to be angry, impatient, and impossible to please. The second child, though, has a close, intimate relationship with her father. She believes Dad to be warm, generous, gentle, and joyful. The first child pictures his father always with a hard scowl on his face; the second child pictures her father with a delighted, ear-to-ear grin on his face. Which child will feel more comfortable taking their true frustrations to their father? The first child will be too careful and fearful of his father; he'll only clean up his feelings so as not to anger Dad. The second child, however, sure of her father's love and goodness, will feel comfortable arguing, demanding answers, and begging for relief. Why? She is secure in her father's love; she knows she won't be cast away for voicing her true feelings. And she knows her father is himself completely secure; he is not anxious over his children's raging. He welcomes them.

When you are frustrated for all the reasons, and you feel like you need to let it out, hear this good news: there's an entire form of prayer for that. As the song goes, "Take it to the Lord in the prayer." For me, this simple truth and strong invitation to pray in lament has shaped me more than any other form of prayer.

My Own Journey of Loss and Anguish

I became acquainted with "these inward trials" at an early age. My earliest set of memories come from when I was six. My youngest sister was born, but all was not well. My dad brought my brother, sister, and me up to the hospital, but little Amy was far behind glass in the NICU. Days later, my parents came home with an empty car seat. Amy lived only a day. The grief and pain were unbelievable. For the next decade, I grew up with the distinct feeling that we were the family that had suffered great loss. At church, my parents' friends and sweet old ladies would come up and hug me. They'd say we were so strong and couldn't believe how we could keep going. At least, I remember thinking, we had suffered such a great loss that it was unlikely another great loss was coming.

But then, when I was sixteen, my brother, who was eighteen, was late coming home from college one day. After many hours, we received a call from a hospital two hours away. There had been an accident. Joseph was flown by helicopter to a trauma center. They could tell us nothing more. So we packed up, climbed in the car, and cried for two hours as we drove into the darkness. After waiting for some time, a group of medical staff called us back into the consultation room. Perhaps you know the room: beige walls, uncomfortable seats, no windows. No good news has ever been shared in this room.

The surgeon told us about Joe's accident, how his car had been hit. He told us, without emotion, that Joe's injuries had been fatal. He almost certainly died on impact. His body was being kept alive on machines, but he was gone. The sheer agony and pain in that moment is still, two decades later, almost unbearable to recall. My mom collapsed, my dad holding her, my sister and I trying to make sense of another sibling gone. For the next two days, we lived and slept in a bare hospital waiting room, with scores of friends and family members making the trip to sit with us and weep with us.

In the years that followed, I struggled with depression, insomnia, and chronic pain. I couldn't sleep, couldn't eat, couldn't study, couldn't play basketball (which was my life at that point). And for a longer season still, I suffered from injuries that took longer than normal to heal, and the depression and physical pain continued. Into my twenties, I got married and went into ministry, and we began having kids. Life was full of joy and work, but grief and depression were always nearby. I had no real understanding of loss and grief, and my body continued to suffer from pain, fatigue, and illness. I was sad and angry almost always, but no one except my wife, Jessie, knew it. As we raised our three boys, watching them play—my oldest is named Joseph, after my brother—was both healing and excruciating. Depression came and went, and at many times I felt I was better off dead. I wasn't suicidal, but I hoped for death to release me from the inconsolable inner anguish. I developed chronic sinus infections, and tried dozens of doctors and treatments to no avail. I could barely sleep. But on I went, pastoring and loving my wife and raising these wild boys.

As I currently prepare to turn forty, I wish I could say the pain has decreased. I've spent countless hours in counseling and spiritual direction, and I've found relief and peace there. My sweet wife has been the most compassionate, patient, and supportive friend imaginable. By God's grace, I have learned to lament, gained balance from a basic depression medication, and found that exercise minimizes the chronic pain.* But still, some days and weeks are still so dark I can barely get out of bed. If it's true that about 40 percent of the Psalms are lament, that's been roughly true of my prayer life as well. I've learned to lament, not through books and lectures, but through the school of hard knocks—tragic loss, living through trauma, and walking with God in the darkness.

Do I long for complete healing? Of course I do. I typically lose about four weeks each year to illnesses, although the last two years, I've lost between eight and ten weeks. My productivity—and

---

* Ironically, I have found that hard exercise—such as competitive cycling, where I push my body to the limit for hours on end, trying to crush and humiliate my friends—minimizes my chronic pain more than anything. It's therapeutic in more ways than one.

I love to be productive—has been massively limited by sickness and depression. Further, I've endured thousands of conversations where well-meaning friends, church members, and strangers have suggested treatments, supplements, doctors, and therapies. There are no quick fixes for pain and suffering, and the wait is exhausting.

But, in the place of my great turmoil, I've also learned a few things. I've learned that I'm not alone. I have felt the presence and nearness of my Father more in times of depression and sickness than during seasons of activity and accomplishment. I'm naturally a very proud, self-assured person; I innately assume that I will win every race, succeed in every endeavor, and overcome every obstacle. But this set of circumstances, I believe, have been given to me by my loving Father to limit my pridefulness and protect me from my sin nature and the darker sides of my personality. Finally, I know that one day I will be healed of all this. In the end, all my grief, inner turmoil, and longsuffering will be only a memory. In fact, it will even increase my joy for all eternity, as I have a source of gratitude that others may lack.

In all this, I think often of Psalm 16. David likely wrote it while fleeing for his life, hiding out in caves, and scrounging for food to survive. As he reflects on his life at the moment, it would be easy for him to curse God and demand answers. But instead, David says, "You are my Lord; apart from you I have no good thing" (v. 2). In the midst of having nothing, he still has everything, because he has the Father's love.

He continues, "Lord, you alone are my portion and my cup; you make my lot secure. The boundary lines have fallen for me in pleasant places; surely I have a delightful inheritance" (vv. 5–6). Now this is a remarkable statement! David understands that he has been given a lot and portion in life, and in this moment, it includes great suffering and loneliness. But because he is so secure in God's love and so joyful in his presence, David can look at his life and say, "this is a good life; I accept the circumstances that God has given me." It's a beautiful statement of spiritual maturity to look on our life's condition, and regardless of how comfortable or awful it seems, to say, "thank you, Lord, for *this* life—the one right in front of me. Peaks, valleys, and all." Our lives are surrounded by boundaries—fences and limitations we have not set in place. Mostly, I want to push back on these limits and try to extend my fences in every direction. Over and over again, the Lord causes me to remain within my boundary lines. Though I rage and wail for a period, eventually I settle in. After a while, I begin to say with David, "You make known to me the path of life; you will fill me with joy in your presence, with eternal pleasures at your right hand" (v. 11).

This, I believe, is the right posture. When our circumstances are brutally difficult, when our life is full of suffering, we can pour out our complaints to the Father. "Why God? How long, O Lord? Why have you abandoned me?" But after some kicking and screaming, we lose our energy. And he is still there. He is still holding us, like a child wailing against his father as he tries to fall asleep. Our heavenly Father keeps holding us, rocking us, gentling singing over us.[13] Eventually, we give up the fight and relax in his care. We know that this life is full of inward trials and profound suffering, but we also discover that we have the one thing we most need—this good and loving Father who surrounds us with his strength and quiets us with his love (Zeph. 3:17).

There Is No Such Thing as Unanswered Prayer

But one question persists. I've spent the majority of this book so far doing everything in my abilities to compel you to seek the Father in prayer. I've been urging you to pour out your heart to him, emphasizing all of Jesus's wild teachings on asking and receiving. Inevitably, that brings up the question of unanswered prayer. Isn't it insensitive to encourage folks to pray with boldness? Isn't it pastoral cruelty to tell stories of answered prayer and urge people to put their faith in God—especially when the results of their prayers may not resolve with such success?

Again, I turn to J. I. Packer. He wrote, "there is no such thing as unanswered prayer."[14] How can this be? This seems like a harsh, untrue statement. But think of it for a moment. First, God is a sovereign Lord, and the whole universe and all of history is under his wise direction and control. Second, God is a good and loving Father, and, like a good parent, he loves us enough to give us what we most need, not merely what we immediately want. As a result, when we pray, "God will either give us what we ask or give us what we would have asked for if we knew everything he knew."[15] This should give us profound comfort. It's an incredible motivation to pray boldly. We can know, because of God's sovereignty and love, that he can and might answer our prayer immediately. Yet we can also know, again because of his sovereignty and love, that he won't give us something that will lead us or others into a worse place.

In my own life, I pray almost every day for my continued struggle with grief, depression, and chronic illness. I pray that God would lift the pain of these things and let me live in more freedom. I can pray this with boldness because I know that God loves me and wants what's best for me—so he might, at any moment, heal me completely. But I can also rest in gratitude each day that my prayer seems unanswered, because I trust that he knows better than I. He desires my spiritual maturity far more than I do. If he answered my prayer the way I wanted him to many years ago, I now realize that it would have decreased my dependence on him. I likely would have gone off my own way in pride and self-sufficiency without this struggle. So, in one sense, he has not answered with a *yes* to my prayer for better mental and physical health. Yet, in another sense, he *has* offered his yes to what I should have been praying for most of all—increased spiritual health and maturity. I still pray for this healing, but I trust that when it doesn't come, his grace is sufficient for me (2 Cor. 12:9).

In other words, unanswered prayer is not the same as God's delayed answer. He always answers our deepest prayers and the prayers we would have prayed if we knew everything he knows and if we loved as purely as he loves. This isn't a motivation to throw up our hands and give up on prayer. It's a motivation to pray. In praying for what we want and need, knowing he may not answer us immediately in the way we want, we learn to pray with both patience and persistence. And all along the way, we are enjoying sweet communion with our Father, living more closely to his heart than if we never struggled and needed him in the first place. We even see this in the prayer life of Jesus, albeit a bit differently.

Praying "Your Will Be Done"

Throughout this book, we've been looking at Jesus's own prayers as a model for our own prayer lives. Does he pray through heartache? Does he lament? Does he wrestle with unanswered prayer? Believe it or not, the answer to all three questions is a resounding *yes*. As the author of Hebrews writes, "During the days of Jesus' life on earth, he offered up prayers and petitions *with fervent cries and tears* to the one who could save him from death, and he was heard because of his reverent submission" (5:7, emphasis added).

The last time we see Jesus praying in the Gospels, he's in the garden of Gethsemane with his disciples. He has just spent the evening with them in the Upper Room, washing their feet and teaching them how to live without him. In these final words, he teaches on prayer, urging them to ask their Father for everything they want and need (John 13–17). Now, it's the early hours of Friday morning, Judas has left to betray him, and Jesus is with his disciples in this garden.

Jesus asks his disciples to stay up and pray with him, telling them, "My soul is overwhelmed with sorrow to the point of death" (Matt. 26:38). Even the Son of God, at his moment of greatest distress, just wanted his friends with him. And yet they couldn't stay up with him. As we already explored briefly, so it will often be for us as well. When we most need others to stay up with us, to join us in our greatest suffering, they won't be able to go with us "deeper into the garden." But don't become angry with them. God will be with you. It may be God's way of getting you alone, on your knees, to give you a greater sense of his goodness and presence.

Jesus proceeds further into the garden to pray alone. As he falls on his face, Jesus pours his heart out to the Father. He prays, "My Father, if it is possible, may this cup be taken from me" (v. 39). The "cup" is an Old Testament symbol for God's wrath. It's an image of judgment, condemnation, and destruction. As Jesus prepares to go to the cross, he is experiencing a level of inner anguish that no other human has experienced before or since. He is about to drink the cup of God's wrath. He is about to take the sins of the world onto himself. He is about to experience the silence of God and bear unspeakable physical pain. Not surprisingly (and not sinfully), he asks God, "Is there any other way?"

But it's here that we learn the power of Jesus's faith, praying through heartache. He doesn't just pray, "may this cup be taken from me." He also prays, "Yet not as I will, but as you will" (v. 39). Even in his moment of greatest suffering, Jesus submitted to God's will. He trusted his Father. He knew there was no other way. But in his humanity, as he poured out his heart honestly, it was all he could think of—some simpler, less painful way out. Knowing this was his Father's plan, though, he submitted. "Not my will, but yours be done."

It wasn't the first time Jesus prayed this. Remember, "Your will be done, on earth as it is in heaven" (Matt. 6:10). He knew he would have to pray this in his own time of need. He knew we'd need to learn this prayer ourselves too. But he didn't just pray it or teach it; he *lived* it. He lived "your will be done" every step of the way. He lived it all the way to the cross, even unto death.

Why did Jesus go through with it? He went to the cross to honor his Father, and he went because he loves us. As the *Jesus Storybook Bible* puts it, "It wasn't the nails that kept Jesus there. It was love."[16] In his great love for us, Jesus identifies with our great pains and needs. He took on humanity, suffered through life in a broken world, experienced horrible grief, heartache, physical pain, rejection, and betrayal. In fact, there's no heartache we experience that he hasn't first experienced (Heb. 4:15).

As John Stott famously wrote, "I couldn't believe in God if it wasn't for the cross. In the real world of pain, how could we worship a God who is immune to it?"[17] When we look at Jesus on the cross, we see a Savior bearing all of our sin to give us his Father in return. When we look at the cross, we see Jesus enduring everything we will suffer in this world—and much more. Have you experienced the loss of a loved one? So has he. Have you been mistreated, oppressed, unjustly marginalized? So has he. Have you been lonely, rejected, betrayed? He has too. Have you suffered great abuse and physical pain? He knows it. And because of all this, he is with us in our suffering.

Our Father is not cruel to expose us to the heartache of our world. He even let his own beloved Son feel it all too. Hebrews 5:8–9 shows us: "Son though he was, [Jesus] learned obedience from what he suffered and, once made perfect, he became the source of eternal salvation for all who obey him." The Father didn't spare his beloved Son from the pain, heartache, and anguish of this world. It was a necessary step in the path from suffering to glory. And if we are truly God's children also, we shouldn't expect to be prevented from affliction. We also are made to walk the path from suffering to glory. And if we suffer like Jesus—by "participation in his sufferings, becoming like him"—we will also experience glory like him— "somehow, attaining to the resurrection" (Phil. 3:10–11). While it's not an easy path, it is the way of Jesus. And thanks be to God: we don't walk it alone.

Every step of the way, our Father remains with us. And at every moment, Jesus knows our agony, walks with us, and intercedes on our behalf. In fact, he suffered the ultimate loss so that we'd never have to. He experienced the Father's silence on the cross ("My God, my God, why have you forsaken me?" Matt. 27:46), so that we'd never have to.

This, exactly this, is why we can pray through heartache. The Father welcomes our complaints and most-honest laments (Jer. 29:12). The Son knows our pain and stands alongside us (Rom. 8:34; 1 John 2:1). The Spirit, too, groans with us (Rom. 8:26–27).

And the Father, the God of all love, promises to wipe away every tear and restore everything that's broken.

So, dear friend, pour out your heart to him. He has made a way for you. He suffered it all for you. He grieves with you in your pain, even now. Don't hold it back. Don't clean it up. Let him have it. In heartache, empty your heart in lament, for he cares for you.

———————

Father,
My heart is broken and swollen with grief.
I have these sorrows deep within me:
My heart is heavy with depression,
I grieve over the death of my siblings and friends,
and I weep over the brokenness of the world.
I feel crushed by the weight of all this.
How long, O Lord?
When will you intervene, when will you set the world right?
Come quickly to save me.
What good is it for me to suffer like this?
I don't understand it and I'm not happy about it.
Yet I trust you.
Come quickly to save me.
Come quickly to remake this world.
In Christ, amen.

7

Cultivating a Hunger for God

Not long ago, an old friend reached out to me. We hadn't had a significant conversation in about fifteen years, and in the meantime, we each got married and had kids, entered our professions, moved a few times, and (I came to learn) suffered more than we thought possible. So, quite randomly, he texts me one day and asked to meet. A few days later, we were sitting over coffee, catching up. Soon, we reached the reason for his text. He explained that he had been going to church for fifteen years, reading his Bible, praying a bit, serving his family, and trying to be a positive witness at work. But for the last few years, everything had gone dry. He had no passion for God. The Scriptures were familiar and lifeless. Prayer was a chore. Service was a struggle. Fellowship was fine, but even that had lost its joy. For six months, his wife had been encouraging him to talk to someone, but he hadn't gotten around to it. Finally, he had reached out to me.

"What do I do?" he asked. "How do I get it back?"

This is perhaps the most common experience I hear in my context, especially among those of us in roughly the middle of life and with a load of church background and experience. People like my friend, who aren't exactly deconstructing their faith, haven't given up on the church, and are still largely doing the stuff. But they're bored, spiritually disconnected, emotionally empty, and disengaged from anything that would resemble passionate New Testament–style life in Christ.

I'm not exactly sure why my old friend thought to reach out to me, but I was happy to connect because I so deeply resonate with his desire. Or, more rightly, his desire for desire. He didn't use the exact words, but the question hanging in the air was: *How do I get my desire for God back? How do I cultivate a hunger for God?*

Like my friend, I'm not content to just go through the motions. I don't want the minimum Christian life, to be assured of my salvation and then go on living life as normal. As a pastor, I don't want a church like this. I don't want to just play church for the next thirty years, retire, and play a lot of golf.* But how do we prevent this? When everything in our world and everything in our flesh is moving us toward complacency, spiritual boredom, lethargy, and lukewarmness, how do we keep the fire burning all these years?

I was in a session with my counselor when he quipped, "You know, hunger is the best sauce." Quickly, he went on to explain something that was probably helpful and timely for me, but I was stuck. Can we go back a few lines? Did you just say, "Hunger is the

---

*Ride my road bike maybe, play pickleball with other graybeards maybe—but my goodness, not golf.

best sauce"? He then explained: If you're hungry, everything tastes a little bit better. If there was a magical sauce you could put on any food and it would make it delicious, well, that's what hunger does for us. It makes everything taste better.

The phrase turned over again and again in my mind. *Hunger is the best sauce.* Have you ever been to a restaurant once, and loved it, but then the next visit is disappointing? Most likely, you were really hungry the first time and not so much the second time. I have done long, demanding bike races, going three or four hours at full speed without anything but electrolytes and a few energy chews. When I get off that bike, collapse on a park bench and someone hands me a couple dry cookies and a protein bar, it's a feast. I've never tasted anything so good in my life! A few dry cookies and an off-brand protein bar become Kansas City barbecue in the presence of strong hunger.

So it is with our spiritual lives. Hunger for God is the best sauce; it sparks a life of prayer, humility, and mission. Living with a true hunger and thirst for God cures every spiritual malady. It moves us to confession and repentance, it moves us toward his Word with expectation, it overflows in praise and thanksgiving. Hungering for God protects us from temptation, softens us to suffering, and enables us to love others purely. When our hearts are filled with a burning, passionate love for God, everything else flows downstream. Saint Augustine put it this way in the fifth century:

> "Give me a man in love; he knows what I mean. Give me one who yearns; give me one who is hungry; give me one far away in this desert, who is thirsty and sighs for the spring of the Eternal country. Give me that sort of man: he knows what I mean."[1]

Ah, for this kind of hunger and thirst! To be men and women of passion, of desire. Oh, to be dissatisfied with the things of this world and to crave first and foremost the presence of God! How many of us have known this hunger, but not for many years? How many of us have never experienced anything of the sort and are skeptical it's even possible? My friend, I appeal to you: not only can this type of passionate hunger exist, it is the ideal state of the mature Christian.

John Piper has written, "There is an appetite for God, and it can be awakened."[2] How do we awaken such a hunger? That's what this chapter aims to do. Seeking God, through prayer, worship, fasting, and other rhythms, enables us to both hunger and thirst for him and to be satisfied in his presence.

One Thing

When you think of women and men in the Scriptures who were hungry for God's presence, who comes to mind? Once again, I come back to David. He was wild, passionate, and fierce in his desires. As a child, he fought bears, lions, and giants. As a young man, he was a musician and poet. As a leader, he was fiercely committed to defending God's name and God's people. He was a warrior and an artist. His passions led him to unbelievable sin, for which there is no excuse. He was a burning, passionate human being. He lived from his heart, and more than anything, he devoted himself to cultivating this hunger for God—not lesser desires.

David's Psalm 27 is my all-time favorite psalm. It's a prayer of single-minded, wholehearted passion for God. The king prays,

> One thing I ask from the LORD,
> this only do I seek:

> that I may dwell in the house of the Lord
> all the days of my life,
> to gaze on the beauty of the Lord
> and to seek him in his temple. (v. 4)

David was a one-thing kind of person. He wasn't satisfied with a thousand inferior desires. He knew only one passion would not lead him astray. He was a man after God's own heart, and he cultivated this heart to actively *seek* the living God. His heart's greatest, truest desire was living in the presence of God.

What we're describing here is true worship. David was a true worshipper. Worship engages our whole being—mind, heart, and will—and focuses us entirely on what is most valuable or important to us. It's possible to do a lot of spiritual activity—singing, praying, reading, and preaching—without really worshipping. You may engage your mind with a book, have a powerful emotional experience, or serve others until great fatigue. But all these things can be done with improper, self-gratifying motives. But true worship engages the whole being around this one wonderful someone or something you value most.

Eugene Peterson has written, "Worship is the strategy by which we interrupt our preoccupation with ourselves and attend to the presence of God."[3] In worship, we clear out everything else and focus on one thing: the presence of God.

In worship, God is the priority, the only priority. I've always been bothered when people use the word *priority* in plural. People ask me, "What are your priorities today?" But the very word means "the *one* thing that matters most." There can only be one priority in your life. If someone came in and looked at your life from the outside, if they followed you moment by moment and could read your thoughts, what would they discover? If you allowed someone (probably with a clipboard) to do a comprehensive 360 audit of your conversations, your calendar, your food intake, your expenses—what might they conclude is your *one* priority?

David's one thing was "that I may dwell in the house of the Lord all the days of my life, to gaze on the beauty of the Lord and to seek him in his temple." David is using three expressions (dwell in God's house, gaze on his beauty, seek him in the temple) to say the same thing: the presence of God. Worship is the act of focusing on the presence and goodness and glory of God. Thus, worship itself is not the goal, it's the act. God himself is the goal; he is what we are worshipping.

When it comes to becoming "one thing" kind-of people, Charles Spurgeon warns us of something that will inhibit us: divided aims. "Divided aims tend to distraction, weakness, disappointment." The Prince of Preachers is saying something profound: when we have divided priorities—multiple things warring inside us for that coveted throne of our heart—we inevitably end up disappointed with the results of our pursuits. Where divided aims ruin us, Spurgeon offers the solution to our problem: "the man of *one* book is eminent, the man of *one* pursuit is successful. Let all our affection be bound up in *one* affection, and that affection set upon heavenly things."[4] Or as Søren Kierkegaard put it, "Purity of heart is to will one thing."[5]

Living with anything else as the priority, our "one thing," will have disastrous results. Many Christians believe in God, obey him, go to church, and read prayer books. Yet they still can't say the Lord is their "one thing." And living with anything else as the priority of our lives, as Tim Keller has said, "will destroy you in the end and disappoint you along the way."[6]

Surely, we'll have to replace whatever else held that sacred place in our lives. As desiring, loving creatures, we never have to create passion, we only have to redirect it. How do we redirect our heart's passion from lesser things to the one true God? How do we hunger for him more than we hunger for all those other divided aims?

Seeking God

David continues in Psalm 27:

> My heart says of you, "Seek his face!"
> Your face, LORD, I will seek. (v. 8)

Here, David is inviting us to pursue God with the strongest of language. To "seek God" is one of the most significant and life-changing themes in all of Scripture. Moses went up the mountain to seek the face of God. The psalmists often say, "I sought the LORD, and he answered me" (Ps. 34:4; see also Ps. 77:2). David prayed, "As the deer pants for streams of water, so my soul pants for you, my God" (Ps. 42:1). Isaiah, like David, was a passionate man who knew how to seek God. He wrote, "My soul yearns for you in the night; in the morning my spirit longs for you" (Isa. 26:9). And later, the prophet said, "I delight greatly in the LORD; my soul rejoices in my God" (Isa. 61:10).

Though it is such a strong theme in the prophets and Psalms, why is seeking God not a more common message in our churches today? I think of my own gospel-centered, Reformed tradition. Our emphasis is, almost always, on God's seeking us. And this is a right and important emphasis. We only seek God because he has first sought us. There is no pursuing God unless he has first pursued us. Even our strongest passion for God is a gift from him. But too often, we can affirm God's initiative toward us without strongly encouraging each other to seek God in response.

The Gospel of John shows us two women and two stories of seeking. In John 4, Jesus sits down at a well in the heat of the day. A Samaritan woman approaches, and Jesus engages her in conversation. First, he says something about "living water," but the woman passes on the offer (v. 10). She seems to say: "Don't worry, I'm not thirsty." But Jesus is working on a deeper level. Of course she's thirsty; everyone's thirsty. Quickly, Jesus identifies that she has been seeking approval and affection in all the wrong places. "Go, call your husband and come back. . . . The fact is, you have had five husbands, and the man you now have is not your husband" (vv. 16–18). (Well, that escalated quickly.)

What's happening here? Jesus knows why she's alone at the well in the heat of the day—the other women in town don't want to be seen with her. Truly, he has shown her that she's desperately thirsty. She's just looking for water in all the wrong places. Jesus has identified her "one thing," and despite all her efforts, it has always run dry. Jesus then makes a beautiful invitation to her: "A time is coming and has now come when the true worshipers will worship the Father in the Spirit and in truth, for they are the kind of worshipers the Father seeks. God is spirit, and his worshipers must worship in the Spirit and in truth" (vv. 23–24). What a profound statement: God is seeking worshippers! He is looking high and low, waiting patiently, searching constantly, for women and men who will worship him. He wants us to worship him, because he knows he is the only one who can truly satisfy us forever. It's a story of a woman who was seeking the wrong thing, and the God who was seeking *her* all along.

John 20 shows us the second woman and the second example of seeking. It's the day of the resurrection, and Mary Magdalene has gone to the tomb (v. 1). When she sees the tomb is empty, she is distraught. She finds the disciples and tells them what she's seen, and they look for themselves. After seeing Jesus's body was not in the tomb, the disciples quickly head back into town. But Mary stays. She keeps waiting, and she keeps seeking. As she waits near the tomb, she weeps. Her Savior, her "one thing," the one who delivered her from profound inner anguish (Luke 8:2), is gone. A moment later, she turns around and notices someone behind her—she assumes it's a gardener.

Jesus asks her the same question he has asked several other people in the book of John. *"Who is it that you're seeking?"* (John 20:15 CSB, emphasis added; see also John 18:4, 7). Mary still doesn't recognize Jesus, but reveals the passion of her single-minded pursuit: "Tell me where you have put [Jesus], and I will get him" (20:15). Finally, Jesus calls her by name. "Mary!" Immediately, she cries out in sheer joy and relief and wonder. She clings to him and weeps freely. See, the moment she reveals she is seeking Jesus, Jesus reveals he is also seeking her. Mary couldn't find Jesus, but as the *Jesus Storybook Bible* puts it, "it was all right. Jesus knew where she was. And he found her."[7] She was the only one brave enough to keep seeking Jesus—all the disciples returned to the city. So, it was to Mary that Jesus first revealed himself after his resurrection. It is a living testimony to the truth of Hebrews 11:6, "he rewards those who earnestly seek him." She sought the Lord, and she found him. Or rather, he found her.[8]

These two seeking stories, held together, show us the beautiful truth: God is seeking us, and we can and must seek him in response. His eyes look throughout the earth for those who are committed to him (2 Chron. 16:9). He wants us; he desires us; he is not satisfied until he has our hearts. In turn, we will never be satisfied until we are satisfied in him. We will go from thing to thing, person to person, activity to busy activity, looking for something to quench our inner thirst. But here is Jesus, standing before us, offering living water. Will you take it? Will you drink from it?

So, yes, we seek God because he first seeks us. In this lifetime, we must cultivate this sort of seeking. We can and must cultivate a hunger for God. Pursuit is a good thing. Expectation is a good thing. Hunger is a good thing. To want only one thing is an eminently good thing. We seek God and cultivate this hunger through prayer, through worship, and also through one more ancient prayer form.

Practice #7: Cultivating a Hunger for God (Fasting)

Growing up in a charismatic-evangelical church, fasting was fairly common but mostly misunderstood. My peers might fast when they had "fallen into sin" and wanted to punish themselves with self-discipline. Others fasted to demonstrate unusual devotion to God. Some others fasted before a big decision or event. Jessie grew up Catholic, so her exposure to fasting was during Lent. Each Lent, she and her friends would pick something to fast from, whether sugar, TV, or cursing. When we met and began dating, we were part of an interdenominational campus ministry, where students occasionally fasted from TV and the internet; these days, the students fast from social media and Netflix. In each tradition, fasting is seen as a dreadful duty, typically done out of rote obedience or shameful self-rejection.

Many years later, as I discovered a more historically-rooted faith (but didn't outgrow my own tradition), I began to see the beauty and power of fasting. Fasting, in a biblical sense, is the elimination of food, temporarily, to focus our appetite on God and his kingdom. Although it's not a common practice today, fasting is a major theme of the Scriptures. It is referenced fifty-five times in the Old Testament and thirty times in the New. Moses fasted, Elijah and the prophets fasted, and David's psalms are often born out of fasting and worship. Jesus fasted forty days before starting his ministry, and the early church fasted regularly.

Several decades ago, Edward Farrell wrote:

> Almost everywhere, at all times, fasting has held a place of great importance since it is closely linked with the intimate sense of religion. Perhaps this is the explanation for the demise of fasting in our day. When the sense of God diminishes, fasting disappears.[9]

That one stings a little. Fasting is an expression of intimacy with God. When our view of God is low, fasting is an afterthought. And yet the inverse is also true: when a sense of God deepens, fasting will likely reappear. We need the discipline of fasting. Why? Three reasons come to mind.

1. Fasting cultivates a hunger for God.

As we have just seen, the one thing in life that David needed was to be in the presence of God. He wanted to see God's beauty and to live close to him. That's the prayer of a person who is hungry for God. The things of this world have lost their taste; nothing else will satisfy. Just this: the presence of the Almighty God—Father, Son, and Holy Spirit. The more deeply you pursue God, live into the Way of Jesus, the hungrier you get for more of his presence. Consider the full quote from John Piper in *A Hunger for God*:

> If you don't feel strong desires for the manifestation of the glory of God, it is not because you have drunk deeply and are satisfied. It is because you have nibbled so long at the table of the world. Your soul is stuffed with small things, and there is no room for the great. God did not create you for this. There is an appetite for God. And it can be awakened.[10]

2. *Fasting purifies our hearts.*

We live in a world of abundance and distraction. We throw more food away each day than some people have access to in their day. And we are surrounded by a thousand other comforts and securities and delicacies. And so, as Mark Sayers puts it, "Fasting is a way to de-secularize our hearts."[11] We might say the most pressing temptations for us are not the things that are purely wrong—rejecting the faith, drinking into drunkenness, viewing pornography. The biggest temptations for us are far more subtle; they're things that are good in moderation, but we go overboard—movies, shows, social media, caffeine, sugar, shopping.

In fasting, we purify our hearts to keep non-essential things from becoming essential. In fasting, we also discover how much our hearts need to be purified. When we're hungry, our anger rises to the surface. We're not angry because we're hungry; it's that we normally feel anger or disappointment or discouragement and throw a hamburger on top of it. Richard Foster writes, "More than any other discipline, fasting reveals the things that control us. This is a wonderful benefit to the true disciple who longs to be transformed into the image of Jesus Christ. We cover up what is inside of us with food and other things."[12]

Fasting helps us discover those sneaky, socially acceptable sins that pile up bit by bit—the ones that we don't even realize weigh us down because we're so used to carrying them. We fast so that we can bring them before God, unburden them from our hearts and backs, and find freedom from them. David said, "I humbled myself with fasting" (Ps. 35:13). Fasting reminds us that we can't live for more than a few weeks without food, a few days without water, a few minutes without air. It reminds us of our need of God. Fasting creates a fresh passion for worship, shows us our need for the support of one another, and reminds us there are people, all over the world and in our own community, who go hungry every day. Fasting makes us hungry to see our friends, coworkers, neighbors, and family members come to feast on Christ.

3. Fasting supports the seeking of God's help.

Throughout Acts, there's a beautiful pattern: Whenever you see a powerful expression of God's Spirit or an effective outreach to a new city or region or a major step forward in the mission of God, turn back a page, and you'll see that the disciples were praying and fasting beforehand. In Acts 9, when Jesus appeared to Saul on the road, he spent the next three days fasting, prior to talking to anyone else or doing anything. In Acts 10, a godly man named Cornelius was praying and fasting, and he receives a vision from God. In Acts 13, the church at Antioch is worshipping, praying, and fasting, and the Spirit says to them, "Set apart for me Barnabas and Saul for the work to which I have called them" (v. 2). In Acts 14, Paul and Barnabas are establishing pastors in each congregation, and all the leaders fasted for a time and committed the new pastors to the Lord.

In our congregation, we have occasionally called for a day (or two or three) of worship, prayer, and fasting to begin a new season or when at a critical transition as a church family. Fasting with others, to cultivate a hunger for God, to purify our hearts, and to seek God's help, is incredibly strengthening.

So how do we get started? It's pretty simple: just don't eat for a while. I have found 24-hour fasts to be the most fruitful. I prefer more, short fasts; others prefer fewer, longer fasts. Either way, when fasting, you normally eat no calories, drink water only, and devote time several times each day to prayer and worship. You may want to let one or two close friends know you'll be fasting—not to brag, but so that you can have some support.

Of course, for some people, fasting from food is unwise. If you are pregnant, diabetic, or have other health issues, you should talk to your doctor before fasting. If you have a history of disordered eating or a complicated relationship to food, you will likely want to abstain from something besides food. If that's you, don't despair, whenever you read "fasting" in this section, just think of something that you can give up for a season to focus on God.

To start a 24-hour fast, eat a normal dinner and don't eat anything before bed. The following day, you may want to have a black coffee if you'll get a headache without any caffeine. Skip breakfast and lunch, trying to drink a glass of water each hour.* If, like

---

* Pro tip: La Croix and other sparkling water can become your best friend while fasting.

me, you have coffee meetings throughout the day, get a hot tea or decaf coffee. Either way, at breakfast and lunch time, use the time you'd normally spend eating instead in prayer and worship. By mid-afternoon, you may be getting hungry, impatient, or distracted. (Around this time, I start having visions of donuts, dancing and mocking me.) This is when fasting is most powerful. Every time you feel hunger, pray to the Lord: "Make me hungry for you, God." Every time you feel irritable or depressed or anything negative, pray: "Father, thank you for showing me this. Come, Lord Jesus." Then at dinner time, 24 hours later, eat again, starting with a light meal. If you're fasting for more than 24–48 hours, you'll want to talk with friends who are experienced in fasting or read one of many good books on fasting—some resources are provided in the endnotes.

Remember the story of Jesus and the Samaritan woman? After a while, Jesus's disciples come back from town and excitedly tell him they've bought food. But Jesus says, "I have food to eat you know nothing about" (John 4:32). The disciples are confused, so he explains, "My food," said Jesus, "is to do the will of him who sent me and to finish his work" (v. 34). Fasting from food is a way of recentering on God's kingdom and our role within it. Jesus's statement demonstrates his "one thing." He can eat and drink at parties. He can also not eat or drink. He can enjoy a lot and can enjoy nothing at all. How? Because he has food the outside world knows nothing about. He is always satisfied with his spiritual food, living in his Father's presence and doing his will.

To return to the earlier John Piper quote: "If you don't feel strong desires for God, it is because you have nibbled so long at the table of the world." Our souls get so easily full on the things of earth, and we struggle to remember the promises of heaven. God didn't create us just for bread and water, but for his presence and his kingdom. Fasting cultivates an appetite for God, purifies our desires, and supports seeking God's face in prayer. If you struggle to make God your priority (which all of us do at some point), fasting is one of the best resources our Father has given us to refocus our hearts on the one thing that matters most.

Wait on the Lord

In one season of life, I spent around eighteen months coming back, again and again, to Psalm 27:4. This "one-thing worship" is what I want to be true of my life. I so desperately wanted to be an unhurried, heart-at-rest sort of person. Or as the poet Wendell Berry put it, "I dream of a quiet man."[13] I don't want to give my life to quick Bible reading, praying for a few minutes, and trying to be a good person. I want to live a quietly passionate life before the *coram Deo*, the face of God. Like David in 2 Samuel 7, I want to be self-forgetful, not caring what others think about me but worshipping God with all my heart, mind, and will.

This is my prayer for my own local church, for the whole global church, and for you as well. May we be a people not caught up in the trappings of modern life—of the pursuit of success or easy circumstances. Let us not be content with popularity among people but barely a relationship with the living God. No, let us seek God's face!

You know, some psalms end with a bold declaration of praise and faith, and others end quietly, in a simple, holding-on faith. How does David's one-thing psalm end?

> I remain confident of this:
> I will see the goodness of the Lord

> in the land of the living.
> Wait for the LORD;
> > be strong and take heart
> > and wait for the LORD. (Ps. 27:13–14)

"Wait for the LORD," we hear so often in the Psalms. Is there anything harder than waiting? Is anything less desirous than fasting? But this man of strong passion said: Be strong, take heart, and wait for the Lord. What does strength have to do with waiting?

Once again, David's circumstances haven't changed. Seeking God doesn't always change our circumstances. But it does give us fresh courage and inner strength. How many of our errors in life have come out of hurry? Instead, David compels us, wait on the Lord for his strength. Waiting on the Lord in faith, seeking him for who he is and not what he can give us, is the ultimate act of inner strength.

But what exactly was David waiting for? He wanted to *see* the goodness of the Lord in the land of the living. David knew that he could lose everything at any point. But he couldn't lose his one thing because he knew he would be with God in the land of the living. This is a common reference to resurrection and eternity, life beyond the grave, which was guaranteed at Jesus's own resurrection.

Here, we have more sweet gospel foreshadowing. David didn't know how this ultimate victory would come, but his whole life pointed to it. He was a shepherd from a poor family, but the Good Shepherd was coming to call all the sheep to himself. He was a warrior who fought Goliath and the Philistines, but a true and better Warrior was coming to finish off Satan, sin, and death forever. David was Israel's anointed, long-awaited king, but the true and better King would come, also from the town of Bethlehem. This King, Jesus Christ, the face of God himself, waited on the Lord like no one else. He hung from the cross as his foes mocked him. Remember, it wasn't the nails that kept him on the cross, it was love. Jesus, in perfect strength, waited until it was finished. He was confident that he would see the goodness of the Lord in the land of the living.

It's because of the life, death, and resurrection of Jesus that all this comes together. Because of Jesus, we as imperfect worshippers could be welcomed into the presence of God. It's in Jesus that David's one thing becomes a sure promise: We will dwell in the house of God all the days of our lives. We will gaze on his beauty and seek him and find him in his heavenly temple. What we experience in part now, we will enjoy in fullness forever.

Suddenly, all the invitations of Jesus and the prophets become clear. Yes, God first seeks us. But he finds us and compels us to come to him in return. In Isaiah 55, the prophet calls out, "Come, all you who are thirsty" (v. 1). But what if we have nothing with us, no righteousness of our own? "Come to the waters; and you who have no money, come, buy and eat!" (v. 1). Come and receive living water.

But we might still say, "I'm weary, I'm tired, I have no strength left." Jesus responds, "Come to me, all you who are weary and burdened, and I will give you rest" (Matt. 11:28). "Come to me," Jesus says.

But we might persist, "I don't feel very hungry or thirsty. I mostly feel dry and bored and empty." On the last and greatest day of the festival, Jesus stood and called out in a loud voice, "Let anyone who is thirsty, come to me!" (John 7:37). By this, he meant the Holy Spirit, who will spark and sustain our hunger and thirst for God.

And on that final day, when heaven and earth meet, and all the sad things come untrue, we will hear one thing. "The Spirit and the bride say, 'Come!'" (Rev. 22:17).

God is seeking worshippers. Jesus is offering you living water. He wants to fill you with his Spirit. He says, "Come to me."

Father,
You have made us for yourself,
and our hearts are restless till they rest in you.
Increase my passion for you, Lord.
Forgive me for settling for broken cisterns
when you offer me living water.
Increase my hunger and thirst for you, one true God.
Let me be satisfied with nothing less.
You are my one thing, my heart's desire.
I remain confident of this:
One day I will see you, and I will be satisfied.
In Christ, my Lord, amen.

8

Prayer as Walking by the Spirit

I know God doesn't make mistakes, but I sometimes wonder if I was supposed to live in the first century. Because I love everything about the early church. Apart from the lack of air conditioning, indoor plumbing, and antibiotics, living in those times would have been amazing. Jesus had just spent forty days with the disciples after his resurrection. He went up and the Spirit came down. Thousands were added to the disciples' number. They worshipped daily, prayed continually, and shared meals together. They cared for widows and orphans, cast out demons, and healed the sick. Even when they were persecuted, they spread out among the nations and planted churches like it was nothing.

But what was it really like? Was it all that great, or were there significant hardships? What was a typical church gathering like? How did they do church in those wild, early years?

In the first thirty years after Jesus's ascension—the period of the book of Acts—the early church was *everything*. It was great, and it was awful; it was evangelistic, and it was legalistic; it was hungry, and it was lukewarm. The only thing it wasn't is *nothing*. Its influence swept the globe in a way no social or religious movement ever has or ever will again.

Early Christianity scholar Michael Green wrote a book with the perfect title, *Thirty Years That Changed the World*. Green puts this season in history like this:

> Three crucial decades in world history. That is all it took. In the years between AD 33 and 64, a new movement was born. In those thirty years it got sufficient growth and credibility to become the largest religion the world has ever seen and to change the lives of hundreds of millions of people. It has spread into every corner of the globe and has more than two billion adherents. It has had an indelible impact on civilization, on culture, on education, on medicine, on freedom and of course on the lives of countless people worldwide. And the seedbed for all this, the time when it took decisive root, was in these three decades. It all began with a dozen men and a handful of women: and then the Spirit came.[1]

Incredible, right? Green goes on to say, "We can and should ask ourselves, 'If those people then acted in the way they did, what are the implications for disciples today, given all the differences brought about by culture, space and time?'"[2]

Among all the unique features of life in the early church, one thing stands out—prayer. If we compare the lifestyle and activities of the early church to our contemporary churches, the single most stark difference will be in our prayer lives. Green writes, "Prayer, not activism, is what they relied on."³ In Acts, prayer is the central power and activity of the church. In chapter 1, we see the believers praying before the coming of the Spirit. In chapter 2, they're gathered together again, almost certainly in prayer, when the Spirit falls. At the end of that wild, historic day, the thousands of new converts are joined to the apostles and early believers together in prayer (Acts 2:42). As chapter 3 opens, we find the believers going up to the temple to pray. This pattern goes on throughout the book. As Green summarizes, the early church had "life-changing power. And it only happened because these men and women put prayer at the top of their priorities."⁴

If prayer was a defining mark of the early church—with beautiful and world-changing results—why has it fallen down the priority list for the church of contemporary America? I believe the answer, as I've repeated a few times already, lies in our general fear that prayer doesn't do much at all. We subconsciously believe we can do more by our intellect, strategies, and efforts than God can do in response to our prayers. How did we get here? There are multiple answers, but I believe one key reason is our diminished emphasis and dependence on the Holy Spirit.

Gospel and Presence

In chapter 1, we said that prayer helps us hold together two beautiful things in tension—*gospel* and *presence*. We don't have to choose one or the other. Embracing the gospel without living for the presence of God can lead us into mere head knowledge and sacrificial living. We can believe in the message of the gospel and have impeccable theology and yet, in the words of Ray Ortlund, barely experience the relational beauty of Christ.[5] Yet, in the same way, living for the presence of God without remaining centered on the gospel can lead us into error as well. We might become focused on spiritual experience, not on knowing God in Christ. Without a heart full of the gospel, our spiritual life can become focused on personal discipline, moral improvement, and self-fulfillment. If you have only the gospel, you have the key to the whole house, but you might never go inside. If you have only the presence, you might have the whole house, but no key to get in.[6]

The Scriptures avoid both errors. The New Testament makes it explicit, and the themes exist in the Old as well. The prophets and apostles are continually holding this out to us. When God sent Moses to speak to Pharaoh, we all remember the famous phrase, "Let my people go" (Exod. 5:1). But we can't miss that the sentence doesn't end there: "Let my people go, that they may worship me in the new land" (author paraphrased). The exodus was setting God's people free *from* oppression and *for* God's presence. We've been drawn out so that we might be drawn in.

Similarly, Paul preaches the gospel to us in Galatians 4:4–6: "God sent his Son . . . to redeem those under the law." But he doesn't end there: "that we might receive adoption to sonship. . . . God sent the Spirit of his Son into our hearts." The gospel sets us free to receive life with God. We're set free *from* and we're set free *for*. Salvation is both redemption *and* communion. Our new life is about being released *and* embraced. It's a once-for-all-time experience, and it's a new-every-day experience.

Just as he called forth Lazarus from the tomb, Jesus calls us out of empty darkness and death and into his own embrace. The invitation for us is to believe in the clear, once-for-all gospel truth and experience its result, a burning passion for the relational presence of God.

The two great Christian movements of the past one hundred years (the evangelical-Reformed tradition and the charismatic movement) have each embraced and championed one of these grand themes. And while both groups certainly affirm both gospel and presence, at least in theory, they have largely run on parallel tracks with little or no overlap practically and relationally. But the early church didn't have this problem. As Paul wrote to the Thessalonians: "For we know, brothers and sisters loved by God, that he has chosen you, because our gospel came to you not simply with words but also with power, with the Holy Spirit and deep conviction" (1 Thess. 1:4–5). Word *and* power. Spirit *and* conviction. Gospel *and* presence.

In this chapter, I want to convince you that prayer does us a double-service, for it is the most practical way we remember God's gospel *and* enjoy God's presence. We learn from the best of the Reformed tradition and the charismatic movement to build holistic, rooted, passionate lives of prayer. We can be both gospel-centered and Spirit-filled in our prayers. To do this, we must understand and experience the Holy Spirit—who he is, what he does, how he comes, and how to live in his empowering presence. Prayer, I believe, is a primary way that we enjoy the embrace of the Father's love, enact our union with Christ, and walk by the Spirit of God.

Life in the Spirit

Put yourself in the sandals of the disciples at the Last Supper. You've been walking with Jesus for three years. What have you experienced? You've heard his teachings. You've witnessed his miracles. You've observed his healings—so many incredible healings. This one, you've discovered, is the true Son of God. But now, as you are gathered around the table by candlelight, he says, "I am going away. I'm leaving. I'm going back to the Father" (John 14:3, 19; 16:16, author paraphrased).

Imagine the confusion. Imagine the immensity of your grief. "What do you mean you're leaving us?" we would ask, just as they did. This is terrible news! How does Jesus respond? He says, "Don't fear. I'm sending you the Advocate, the Holy Spirit. He will be in you. He will remind you of everything I've said. He will give you peace" (John 16:13–15, 33, author paraphrased). It's his clearest and most important teaching on the Holy Spirit, and yet it remains challenging, confusing, and overwhelming to us today.

Further, Jesus says, "I am going away. But I won't leave you alone. I will give you the Spirit, and he will be in you" (John 14:18, author paraphrased). And as he says in John 16:7: "Very truly I tell you, it is for your good that I am going away. Unless I go away, the Advocate will not come to you; but if I go, I will send him to you."

How could this be? How could it be better for Jesus to not be on earth? Because *it's better to have Jesus within each and every one of us than to have him just in one place.* Instead of Jesus being locally constrained to one place on the map, it's better to have the Spirit of Christ, the Spirit of God, within every single Christian all across the globe. On top of that, as long as Jesus was still on earth, his disciples didn't have access to life in the Spirit.

Prayer as Walking by the Spirit

Fast-forward to the other side of the cross and resurrection. Now that Jesus has died, risen, and ascended into heaven, he has sent his Spirit. We are filled with his presence the moment we believe in him. In that very moment, we enter into life in the Spirit.

When Jesus goes to the Father, it begins a new age, the age of the Spirit descending on his people. As Spirit-filled Christians, we are in him and he is in us. We will cover the earth, doing the same things Jesus did—teaching, building relationships, caring for the sick, encouraging the weary, and lifting up the poor. What Jesus would do in a single time and place during his earthly life, his followers now do generation after generation, all across the globe. His work is no longer bound to Jerusalem, Galilee, and the surrounding areas. With the Holy Spirit enlivening God's global church, Christ's work is now happening *everywhere*—even "to the ends of the earth" (Acts 1:8).

Indeed, we are continuing the ministry of Jesus as we live by the Spirit and in his kingdom. The book of Acts was written by Luke, and at the very beginning of Acts, he references his first volume (which we just call Luke), and he says it was "all that Jesus began to do and to teach until the day he was taken up to heaven" (Acts 1:1–2). By implication, he means that Acts—the story of the early church—is all that Jesus *continues to do* through his followers on earth. Throughout Acts, we see Jesus's followers doing everything that he himself did: healing the sick, preaching and teaching, challenging religious leaders, hearing God's voice, and even raising the dead. And there's nothing in Scripture to suggest God intended that only for first-century believers. Rather, everything in Scripture states that we should hope, anticipate, and pray for everything that happened in Jesus's ministry and in the book of Acts to continue today, by the power of the Holy Spirit. This is how we "will do even greater things" than Jesus did (John 14:12), because we are all continuing Jesus's ministry, all over the world.

By "life in the Spirit," we mean all the activities that the Holy Spirit fulfills in and through us. He works uniquely in us to produce a certain kind of life. This list below is what it looks like:

Life in the Spirit

Praising God the Father and Jesus Christ in the power of the Spirit

Being reborn by the Spirit, experiencing new birth and baptism in the Spirit

Growing into Christ's likeness through the Spirit

Worshipping God in the power and freedom of the Spirit

Praying to God with both contemplative peace and bold expectancy

Belonging to a local church, infused with Spirit-filled people

Serving that community with your Spirit-given gifts (mercy, service, teaching, administration, faith, prophecy, tongues, interpretation, healing, and so on)

Seeking God's face and his presence and power

Sharing the good news about God's grace and love with others, in faith that the Spirit of God may change their hearts and renew their souls

Longing for the return of Christ, when Satan, sin, and death are forever defeated, heaven and earth are joined as one, and we live forever with resurrection bodies in the light of God's face in the new creation

For me, this is the stuff. I didn't become a Christian simply because I wanted assurance that I won't go to hell when I die. Christianity is not about following the rules and becoming a better person. It's not even about having perfect theology and serving in a great church. Christianity is truth *and* experience; it's gospel *and* presence. It's about walking out of the smelly old tomb, stepping into the light, and receiving the embrace of our friend, Jesus.

We're not on earth to get things done for God. He's not nervous about the current state of things, and he is not uncertain about the future. He is seated on the throne—not pacing nervously, not looking around for his battle gear, not calling out constant commands to his people. He's comfortable. Things, believe it or not, are unfolding exactly according to his plan.

No, life in Christ, by the Spirit, is not about getting stuff done; it's about seeing our hearts transformed. Eternal life is about being caught up in something bigger than ourselves. Life in the kingdom is about joyfully participating in the work of God in a place we love. This is life in the Spirit: living together in God's presence, in the shining light of his face.

It's interesting how much time the apostle Paul spent instructing the early churches in the presence and power of the Holy Spirit. In Ephesians 5:18–20 he writes, "Do not get drunk on wine, which leads to debauchery. Instead, be filled with the Spirit, speaking to one another with psalms, hymns, and songs from the Spirit. Sing and make music from your heart to the Lord, always giving thanks to God the Father for everything, in the name of our Lord Jesus Christ."

To be drunk is to be under the influence of an outside substance. When one is drunk (which Paul clearly rejects), the alcohol in their system tends to minimize their sense of fear and hesitation; they say things they wouldn't normally say and get themselves in situations they wouldn't otherwise be in. In the same way, being full of the Spirit is being under the influence of another. The person of the Holy Spirit reminds us of our security in the Father's love. He minimizes our fear and hesitation. We say things we wouldn't normally say—we become bolder with the gospel. We find ourselves in situations we wouldn't normally be in—spreading the gospel and building communities all over the globe.

But another, even more important thing, stands out here. Paul commands the Ephesian believers to "be filled with the Spirit" just moments after reminding them that they *already have the Spirit*. In fact, Paul has already referenced the Spirit's presence in their lives multiple times. The Ephesian believers are sealed with the Spirit (1:13), have access to the Spirit of wisdom and revelation (1:17), approach the Father by the Spirit (2:22), understand the Scriptures through the Spirit (3:5), gain strength in their inner beings through the Spirit (3:16), keep the unity of the Spirit together (4:3–4), and have the potential to grieve the Spirit (4:30). So, clearly, Paul is going to great lengths to demonstrate how the Spirit is already at work in these believers. Why, after all that, would he compel them to "be filled with the Spirit" (5:18)?

While some charismatic believers view this verse as support for a second, post-regeneration baptism in the Spirit, it seems more likely that Paul is simply compelling them to receive more of the Spirit they already have. Francis Schaeffer explains it like this:

> Though we are indwelt by the Holy Spirit immediately when we accept Christ as Savior, *being indwelt is not the same as having the fullness of the power of the Holy Spirit*. The disciples had to wait to receive the Spirit at Pentecost. Christians today are to follow the same order: to be indwelt by the

Holy Spirit at salvation and to know something of the reality of the power of Christ through the agency of the Holy Spirit—and then to work and witness. The order cannot be reversed. There are to be many fillings.[7]

This reality has far-reaching implications for our prayer lives. We receive the personal, empowering presence of the Holy Spirit the moment we put faith in Christ, but we also have access to more of the Spirit's presence and power throughout our lives. Indeed, this is why God longs to give us *more* of the Holy Spirit (Luke 11:13). He never leaves us, but our experience of him wanes and diminishes. Our role is to continually seek a greater awareness of his presence and a greater measure of his fullness within us. It is right, therefore, to pray as the early church prayed, "Come, Holy Spirit."[8] What, then, would a more Spirit-filled prayer life look like?

Prayer and the Spirit of God

A life of walking by the Spirit is a life of prayer, and a life of prayer is a life of walking by the Spirit. Prayer is a refusal to do life in our own strength and ingenuity. It's a plea for help from above (and within). Prayer demonstrates a heart that is hungry for God's presence and intervention in our world. In the same way, walking by the Spirit is a lifestyle of depending on God, not self, for life and breath. The two things are nearly synonymous.

To the Galatians, Paul wrote:

> Walk by the Spirit, and you will not gratify the desires of the flesh. . . . If you are led by the Spirit, you are not under the law. . . . But the fruit of

the Spirit is love, joy, peace, forbearance, kindness, goodness, faithfulness, gentleness and self-control. Against such things there is no law. Those who belong to Christ Jesus have crucified the flesh with its passions and desires. Since we live by the Spirit, let us keep in step with the Spirit. (Gal. 5:16, 18, 22–25)

Paul compels us to become like Christ, developing the same character of Jesus and demonstrating his characteristics. The way we become like Christ is by walking in the Spirit, living by the Spirit, and keeping in step with the Spirit. These three phrases suggest a practical, ongoing, moment-by-moment relationship with the Holy Spirit. It is only through this perpetual dependence on the Spirit that we can uproot the power of sin in our lives and demonstrate Christlikeness.

Dependence is a key word there. As we've seen, our human tendency is to rely on ourselves, defend ourselves, and promote ourselves. Once more, Schaeffer says it poignantly:

> The central problem of our age is not liberalism or modernism, nor Roman Catholicism . . . nor the threat of communism, nor even the threat of rationalism . . . nor, I would add, postmodernism, consumerism, or [other more contemporary isms]. . . . The real problem is this: the church of the Lord Jesus Christ, individually or corporately, tending to do the Lord's work in the power of the flesh rather than of the Spirit. The central problem is always in the midst of the people of God, not in the circumstances surrounding them.[9]

This happens both individually and together in the church. Our lives, apart from walking by the Spirit, become an anxious experiment in self-reliance. We become devoted to building and protecting our own little kingdoms. We don't intend this, but when our old self (what Paul calls the flesh) is more active than our new self (who we are in Christ), we live no differently from our non-Christian neighbors. Our churches and ministries can operate the same way. We drift back into our old self-reliant selves collectively, and we end up busy, distracted, and focused on building a spiritual empire (however big or small) that is not the kingdom of Christ. We ought to honestly ask: If the Holy Spirit suddenly left our ministries, how long would it take us to notice? If our prayers suddenly were ineffective, would our ministries come to a grinding halt? Or would they continue undiminished—because it wasn't dependent on the Spirit and prayer to begin with?

I have often told my congregation that I don't want to spend the next thirty years playing church. I don't want to go through the motions. I don't want to just preach sermons, meet needs, and care for the flock—although I do want to do all those things. I want *more*. I want to be part of what Jesus is doing in the world in the twenty-first century.

In Galatians, the old apostle knows this self-assured, fleshy habit within us and wants to sever it. He wants us to replace it with Spirit dependence. What would such a walking by the Spirit look like? The most practical, moment-by-moment way to keep in step with the Spirit is through an ongoing conversation with the Father. Through God's Son, by the power of God's Spirit who indwells us, we can continually praise our Father God, humble ourselves before him, seek to do his will, and ask for all that we need and want. Prayer is the heart of walking by the Spirit.

But does this mean that living by the Spirit will mean we become lazy people and get less done? Not at all, says Schaeffer. "The truth is that by doing the Lord's work in the Lord's way, we will accomplish more not less," he writes. "You need not fear that if you wait for God's Spirit you will not get as much done as if you charge ahead in the flesh. After all, who can do the most, you or the God of heaven and earth?"[10]

Walking by the Spirit means continually recognizing and rejecting our own self-sufficiency, and there's an ancient prayer practice that enables us to do just that.

Practice #8: Giving Up Control of Your Life (Surrender)

Surrender is a discipline of prayer that is more of an internal posture than an exact form. The mere word *surrender* might even evoke feelings of discomfort, distrust, and fear. I've even heard believers say we should never use the word *surrender* because it immediately raises so many negative emotions. I understand the impulse here; countless friends of mine have been neglected, marginalized, or oppressed by others in positions of authority over them. But surrendering to God does not mean entering into unsafe territory or losing your own agency in life. In fact, nothing is safer or more lifegiving than surrendering our lives to our heavenly Father.

The late pastor and author Jack Miller writes:

> We have an obsessive need to feel in control of our lives. Such a hunger is a primary obstacle to the Spirit's working mightily in us and through us. Busyness is a hindrance to fellowship with the Lord. But what lies beneath our need to fill up

every last moment with activity? The answer is that we want to be in charge of our lives, and our constant activity gives us the feeling we are mastering our world. . . . Why, then, is the Holy Spirit not leading more of us into a maximum Christian life? The answer is that we are letting him have only a minimal control of our life choices. . . . Above all, the Spirit is leading us to discover empowerment through giving up control of our lives. He is calling for complete surrender daily.[11]

The Spirit "is calling for complete surrender daily." And he does this because he knows it's exactly what we most need. This is the paradox of Christianity, the heart of so many of Jesus's teachings and parables. Blessed are the meek. Humility is the key to greatness. Weakness is the way to true strength. The way to find your life is to give it away. In the same way, if we try to control our lives, we'll always tend toward hurry, anxiousness, anger, and bitterness. But if we surrender ourselves to God's loving and strong care, by submitting to and following the Spirit, we'll discover peace and continual renewal. (Even more, we'll use our God-given agency in redemptive ways.)

In prayer, surrender looks like a combination of adoration, confession, contemplation, and petition. We might begin by praising God and reorienting our hearts to him. Then, we might sit silently, searching our thoughts and the past few days to recognize where we've relied on our own skills, intellect, or energies instead of depending on the Spirit. We can then specifically seek the Father's forgiveness and release each situation or relationship to him. It could look like this: "Father, yesterday I became angry when one of my coworkers joked about one of my ministry areas being disorganized. I also became defensive when Jessie asked me to help the boys get ready in the mornings before school. I recognize also that I spent hours working without turning to you in prayer even once. Forgive me for all this self-reliance. Soften my heart, help me remember that you are a good and patient Father, so I can be more present to the boys and better embody your character. Help me turn to you—the one who is always available with fresh mercies—more continually tomorrow. Thank you, Lord. Amen."

As we become more comfortable in prayers of surrender, it becomes easier to face each day's challenges. It becomes second nature to seek God's strength when our kids are difficult, when a coworker subtly insults us, and when someone cuts us off in traffic. Remember, the love of God makes us radically secure. We have nothing to prove and defend. Every day, we'll make mistakes and not fully walk by the Spirit. But we're still children of God, and he is still pleased with us—because he sees his own Son and Spirit working in us. Indeed, this is one final role of the Spirit that can transform our prayer lives.

Let's close this chapter by meditating on a single thought: the Spirit opens us to the Father's love. Moments before the Galatians passage we've been considering, Paul writes this:

> But when the set time had fully come, God sent his Son, born of a woman, born under the law, to redeem those under the law, that we might receive adoption to sonship. Because you are his sons, God sent the Spirit of his Son into our hearts, the Spirit who calls out, "*Abba*, Father." (Gal. 4:4–6)

This is both gospel and presence. God sent his Son to pay the debt of our sins, to draw us back to himself. To make us sons and daughters. It doesn't matter what you've done. It doesn't matter how long it's been since you turned to him. It doesn't matter what's been done to you—he will begin to heal and restore all that too. He's pouring out his love on you, he's pouring out his Spirit on you.

He's done all the work. There's nothing left to do. All we bring to this relationship is our need of him. This is the Father, standing on the porch every evening, waiting for his prodigal sons and daughters. And when finally we come back home, oh, he runs to meet us! He has made a way for us. Not just a way out of trouble, but a way back to himself. He draws us out to draw us in. He sets us free to embrace us forever.

The Spirit opens us to the Father's love. We don't have to do life in our own strength anymore. We have the presence and power of God within us forever. Nothing could be safer and smarter than surrendering to him completely and continually.

Holy Spirit,
We praise you, holy God, and call on your name.
We confess our sin where we have neglected you,
and we seek your forgiveness where we have grieved you.
Spirit of God, let us know you rightly
and experience you deeply.
Open us to the Father's love, focus our eyes on Christ,
and let us walk by your presence and power.
We humbly seek more of you.

Come and fill our hearts, minds, and churches with your power.
Come, Holy Spirit!
In Christ, amen.

9

In the End, Everything Turns to Praise

Gratitude is one of the most powerful forces in human experience. "A review of 70 studies and more than 25,000 people revealed a direct correlation between higher levels of gratitude and lower levels of stress, depression, and anxiety."[1] One study published in 2021 found that a "gratitude intervention" (keeping track of things to be thankful for five days per week) led to significant and lasting improvements in mental health and well-being in just six weeks.[2] Other studies have shown that practicing gratitude improves the quality of sleep and diminishes the risk of heart disease.[3]

Gratitude is having its day in our culture, and with good reason. However, this comes to no surprise for those of us in the Christian tradition. The Psalms especially lay out a pattern of thanksgiving that invites us into a deeper and more satisfying life. Jesus taught that gratitude demonstrates true faith and is a feature of a deeply changed life (Luke 17:11–19). Almost every one of Paul's letters begin and end with overflowing thanksgiving. (Although not a perfect definition, gratitude is a posture or disposition, while thanksgiving is the act of expressing gratitude.)

As the thirteenth-century monk Meister Eckhart supposedly wrote, "If the only prayer you say in your life is 'thank you,' it will be enough."[4] As novelist Morris West has said, "at a certain age our lives simplify and we need have only three phrases left in our spiritual vocabulary, *Thank you! Thank you! Thank you!*"[5] When we practice thanksgiving, we begin to see just how many of our prayers are answered and we can begin to understand why some of our prayers *aren't* answered. Thanksgiving is the posture and practice of mature faith. In a soft heart, thanksgiving flows naturally. In a hard, busy, or fearful heart, thanksgiving requires prayer and practice.

In a similar way, celebration is both an overflow of a joyful heart and a discipline to be cultivated. Celebration and gratitude are dear friends. Thanksgiving is an expression of joyful gratitude; a celebration of the life and gifts God has given us.

In a sense, nothing is more natural than celebration. When something goes our way, celebration is a sudden and natural explosion. Even one who isn't grateful will still find things to celebrate. I'm a sports guy (if you didn't pick that up already). When I'm at a Missouri basketball game with my boys, I don't have to tell myself to celebrate a three-pointer. Instinctively, every fan in the arena celebrates at once.

But most of the time, especially in our spiritual life, celebration and gratitude are disciplines. We must learn to celebrate spiritually and give thanks in everything.

In my church tradition, we have enjoyed a rediscovery of the importance of lament. As we have seen, lament is a crucial element of prayer and an appropriate posture of biblical spirituality. Many decades of church life did not make space for lament, grief, and sadness, and I'm so grateful it's been recovered. But I wonder if, in our recovery of lament, we've lost an appreciation for Christ-centered celebration and thanksgiving. In my own tribe of churches, I fear that many of us pastors and churches have overreacted. We now struggle to be joyful, to be thankful, and to celebrate the life God has given.

Lament is meant to give way to joy, gratitude, contentment, and celebration. A life of lament only is an incomplete life. It gives an inaccurate picture of Jesus-shaped Christianity. Yes, he was a Man of Sorrows (Isa. 53:3 KJV), but he was also the most joyful person to ever live (John 15:11). He embodied the full spectrum of human experience—laughing and crying, joking and grieving, feasting and fasting, friendship and aloneness, pleasure and pain. To accept only half of Christ's emotional life is to reject half of what he came to welcome us into. We should reject neither lament nor celebration. We should embrace both, and experience the fullness of life, whatever it brings, on this side of the resurrection. As one thinker wrote, we thank our Creator by enjoying our lives.[6]

In this final chapter, let's consider how we can practice a life of celebration, learn to practice thanksgiving, and see that, in the end, all of life turns to praise.

The Biblical Story Is a Celebration Story

From beginning to end, the biblical narrative is a celebration story. God delights in his creation and says it is "very good" (Gen. 1:31). Adam breaks out in the world's first love song when he is given his wife, Eve (Gen. 2:23). Centuries later, the exodus narrative is a story of freedom and festival. When Moses demanded freedom from Pharaoh, it was "because we are to celebrate a festival to the Lord" (Exod. 10:9). Indeed, when God provided freedom, the first thing Israel did was to stop and celebrate God's provision (Exod. 12). Later, God's laws through Moses include dozens of commands to celebrate festivals (e.g., Exod. 23; Deut. 16).*

The next high point of Israel's history comes under King David, another champion of celebration. When David brought the ark of the covenant back to Jerusalem, he celebrated with all his might before the Lord (2 Sam. 6:21). The psalms of David and his companions are full of songs of celebration and thanksgiving. We are commanded to celebrate: "Serve the Lord with fear and celebrate his rule with trembling" (Ps. 2:11). Psalm 89 says those who fear God "rejoice in [his] name all day long; they celebrate [his] righteousness" (v. 16). Psalm 145 agrees: "One generation commends your works to another. . . . They celebrate your abundant goodness and joyfully sing of your righteousness" (vv. 4, 7).

Israel's revivals all include an element of celebration. In 2 Chronicles 30, the revival under Josiah restored a celebration of the Passover and other festivals. And it sounds like quite a party: "none of the kings of Israel had ever celebrated such a Passover as did Josiah" (2 Chron. 35:18). And if the Bible says someone knows how to party, that's something. The revival under Ezra and Nehemiah brought conviction of sin, but then Ezra commanded them to stop mourning and celebrate (Ezra 3:4; 6:16). When God's Word revives us, we are moved to celebration: "Then all the people went away to eat and drink, to send portions of food and to

---

* Next time someone complains about all the laws in the Bible, remind them how many of God's commandments are to observe feasts and festivals, and how many times God commands us to enjoy our lives.

celebrate with great joy, because they now understood the words that had been made known to them" (Neh. 8:12). Again, it sounds like a party: "From the days of Joshua son of Nun until that day, the Israelites had not celebrated it like this. And their joy was very great" (v. 17). In other words, Josiah held the crown for a while, but centuries later, these Israelites took it to the next level.

Then there's Jesus, and no one can outdo Jesus when it comes to celebrating. Jesus's parables demonstrate an abundance of celebration. A shepherd loses a sheep and finds it again. To celebrate? A group of friends gather and rejoice together. A woman loses a coin and likewise finds it again. To celebrate? Get the gang together again because it's time for another party. A father gives away half his estate as an inheritance to an ungrateful son, then welcomes that very same son back when he returns, even when the inheritance was wasted. To celebrate? The father decides to throw a massive party with a fattened calf. Oh, and with all three scenarios of a lost thing being found again, don't forget the point: *this is what happens in heaven when one lost person returns to the Lord.* The steak is on the table, the music is turned up, and the sandals come off. Why would God be so extravagant over just one sheep, just one coin, just one son? He says, "we had to celebrate and be glad, because this brother of yours was dead and is alive again; he was lost and is found" (Luke 15:32). According to God, he *has to* celebrate certain things.

Those aren't the only stories where we see God being extravagant. Even when a party isn't at hand, we see the Father's abundant nature on full display in other stories Jesus tells about him. A king forgives a man's debt of ten thousand talents. A vineyard owner pays his workers far more than they deserved. A king gives wedding invitations to every poor person and outcast in all the land, knowing they can't pay back anything. As Andrew Wilson notes in *Spirit and Sacrament*, "it is hard to think of a parable in which a God-figure features and he is not characterized by giving away more than he should."⁷ Jesus's point is simple: Our Father loves to give, to bless, and to celebrate in abundance. He's got more than enough to go around, and he's not afraid of all-out partying.

Jesus's life, death, and resurrection is the focus of celebration for the New Testament church. The coming birth of Jesus is described as "good news that will cause great joy for all the people" (Luke 2:10). When the gospel reaches Samaria, "there was great joy in that city" (Acts 8:8). When the gospel reaches Pisidian Antioch, "the disciples were filled with joy and with the Holy Spirit" (Acts 13:52). When the jailer was converted under Paul's evangelism, "he was filled with joy because he had come to believe in God" (Acts 16:34). Indeed, the church-Spirit age, between Jesus's resurrection and his second coming, is to be an age of joy. As Jesus told his disciples before his death, "Very truly I tell you . . . you will grieve, but your grief will turn to joy" (John 16:20).

All this is a strong foundation for the apostle Paul's strong commands to celebration and thanksgiving. He writes, "Rejoice in the Lord always. I will say it again: Rejoice!" (Phil. 4:4). And "Rejoice always, pray continually, give thanks in all circumstances; for this is God's will for you in Christ Jesus" (1 Thess. 5:16–18).

How, then, do we cultivate a spirit of gladness, peace, and celebration? The pathway there is simple: prayers of thanksgiving lead us, sooner or later, into festival joy.

Practice #9: The Path to Joy and Celebration (Thanksgiving)

Some prayer practices are difficult to learn. Wise and humble saints have spent their lives learning the practice of contemplation and to continually surrender their lives to God. But we're closing these prayer practices with the simplest one possible: thanksgiving. It's so simple, in fact, that a university study could ask their students to participate in a "gratitude intervention," simply asking them to write down things for which they're grateful. In other words, thanksgiving is one of the most powerful, most important practices of prayer, but it can also be learned by a three-year-old. "What are you thankful for, Jack?" "My dog, my stuffed bear, and my dad." Well done, good and faithful servant.

Though it doesn't take a rocket scientist or monk living in the hills of Tuscany, there is a pattern to follow for thanksgiving. It has helped give a bit of structure to my life of spiritual gratitude. First, after quieting your heart and reorienting to God, make a simple list of what you're thankful for. This is a list of gifts from the Lord, ways he's provided, and little pleasures from your day or week. It's essentially a list of basic stuff, but it's a good place to begin. Write down twenty things you're thankful for.

Now, this first step can be done by a non-Christian or a three-year-old, so consider this next step. Second, prayerfully remember the One who has blessed you in these ways. Write out what your grateful list shows you about God's character and love. Taken together, the two steps might look like this:

> Father, thank you that I didn't have any nightmares and woke up feeling refreshed. You are the

God who protects my mind and restores my soul. You never sleep. You are always faithful.

Father, thank you that my first meeting of the day went well, and this project is off to a good start. Lord, you are in sovereign control of the universe, whether or not my stuff is going well. Regardless of the success of my work, you are pleased with me.

Father, thank you that my daughter is recovering from her sickness. You are the God who heals, whether by miracle or by medicine or by the design of our bodies. Praise you, Lord God, creator, sustainer, and healer.

Father, thank you for this Sunday gathering with the church. It is such a joy to worship and enjoy fellowship among your people. You are the God who "sets the lonely in families" (Ps. 68:6), and you never leave us or forsake us.

Thanksgiving is both simple and profound. In fact, thanksgiving is so simple, at multiple occasions, I thought of removing this section altogether. As I looked back through the last few prayer books I've read (each recently published), I couldn't find a single chapter or section on thanksgiving. But turning to the classic eight volumes by E. M. Bounds, I found a beautiful emphasis on thanksgiving in prayer that reminded me it's too important to be left out. Why? Because thanksgiving is a primary weapon against skepticism, cynicism, and complaining against God. (Remember, there's a difference between complaining about life to God like the psalmists and complaining against God.) In his second volume, *The Essentials of Prayer*, Bounds writes that "Gratitude and thanksgiving forever stand opposed to all murmurings at God's dealings with us, and all complaining at our lot. Gratitude and murmuring never abide in the same heart at the same time. . . . Appreciative men and women have neither the time nor disposition to stop and complain."[8] And later, Bounds concludes, "True prayer and gratitude lead to full consecration, and consecration leads to more praying and better praying. A consecrated life is a life of both prayer and thanksgiving."[9]

Simple and profound. Thanksgiving can be practiced by a child, and it can sustain us in our dying days. We would do well for our first and last words to be simply "Thank you, thank you, thank you." And, although thanksgiving is a worthy practice in itself, it also leads us into something else rare and wonderful.

The Secret of Contentment

Contentment is one of the classic virtues of the Christian life, but it is not spoken of as frequently as it once was. In previous generations, contentment was a sort of crowning virtue, one reached at the end of a long life of pursuing Christ. But these days, especially in affluent America, teaching on contentment can get a pastor fired. What is contentment?

When Paul writes of "contentment" in his letters, he uses a Greek word that is a combination of the words *full* and *soul*. To be content is to have a full soul. It's not a soul that's full *of* itself; it's a soul that's full *by* itself. Contentment is the soul's state of having no further need. Paul writes, "godliness with contentment is great gain. For we brought nothing into the world, and we can take nothing out of it. But if we have food and clothing, we will be content with that" (1 Tim. 6:6–8).

Paul is writing in the context of money, simplicity, and generosity, but at the deepest level, he's writing about true satisfaction. He knows, like Jesus explained to the woman at the well, true satisfaction is available in this life. True freedom is possible. Our culture describes freedom as personal autonomy, having no needs, and the power to buy anything. But true freedom is acknowledging our needs, relying on others, and the power to not need anything more. Contentment is true freedom.

As Paul put it, "I have learned the secret of being content in any and every situation, whether well fed or hungry, whether living in plenty or in want. I can do all this through him who gives me strength" (Phil. 4:12–13). The secret of contentment is to rely not on ourselves but to live and do all things "through him who gives me strength." The good life is not found in accumulation, comfort, or status. The truly good life is dwelling in the presence of God and gaining fresh strength from him. Indeed, the secret of contentment is the *source* of contentment—God himself. As C. S. Lewis put it, "he who has God and everything else has no more than he who has God only."[10] Or in the Bible's words: "The LORD is my shepherd; I have all that I need" (Ps. 23:1 NLT).

As we said many pages ago, we've been lied to our whole lives. We've been told that everything depends on us. We've been taught that if we want something, we have to work for it. We've learned to hustle and grind and make things happen. And further, if you have something, you better hold it tightly, because if you lose it, you'll never get it back. All these messages make sense in a world without a good and loving Father. These things make sense in a world of scarcity. But we do have a good and loving Father. And his world is a world of abundance, not scarcity. He is the giver of every good gift, and as we see in the wedding at Cana, the feeding of the five thousand, and in the resurrection and new creation, God loves to give abundantly, hilariously over the top. He's our Father, our provider, our shepherd. And if God is my shepherd, as Dallas Willard said, "the world is a perfectly good and safe place to be."[11]

See, prayer keeps us in touch with the God who gives and gives and gives. Prayer is our lifeline to the Spirit's presence and power. Prayer is our continual surrender to the One who loves us and provides for us. We can live in true freedom; we can live in blissful contentment. We can be who we are, where we are, and know that we have all that we need. As poet and novelist Wendell Berry wrote in *Hannah Coulter*,

> You mustn't wish for another life. You mustn't want to be somebody else. What you must do is this:
>
> "Rejoice evermore.
> Pray without ceasing.
> In everything give thanks."
>
> I am not all the way capable of so much, but those are the right instructions.[12]

Yes, they are. Celebration, thanksgiving, and contentment are where prayer leads us. It is a long and winding journey, fraught with troubles on all sides, but we'll get there eventually. That doesn't mean prayer is easy. It's not. But as my friend John Starke writes, "A vibrant prayer life is possible for you. I know it may not seem this way, but the whole thing is rigged for triumph."[13] I love that phrase. It's rigged because we are children of God. We are deeply and completely loved by our heavenly Father. Prayer is a wildly good gift from God, a continuous conversation between God's heart and ours. And when we've been praying for any amount of time, we'll find ourselves enjoying his presence, celebrating this life he's given, and eventually, all our prayers simply become praise.

In the End, Everything Turns to Praise

When I was living and pastoring in Louisville, Kentucky, I used to spend my Friday mornings away from the office, reading, studying, and praying. (It's a rhythm I continue today, and I've added Tuesday mornings too.) I used to get to Anchorage Café the moment it opened, then find a comfortable chair near a window on the lower level. I remember sitting there one morning, worn out and discouraged, and opening an older book by Eugene Peterson. It's called *Answering God: The Psalms as Tools for Prayer*, and I can remember with vivid, emotional clarity reading his closing chapter. Peterson shows how the overall arc of the Psalter leads us through the range of human experience but settles in a certain place. In the end, at Psalm 150, after all these laments and petitions, the final word belongs to praise. In the end, everything turns to praise.

The Book of Psalms is divided into five smaller books. You'll see these headings in your Bibles: Book I (Psalms 1–41), Book II (Psalms 42–71), and so on. While I don't often pay attention to which of the five books I'm currently in, the order of these books and the nature of how each one ends provides a powerful clue to prayer. While there are many themes found throughout the Psalms, each of the five books end with a so-called "hallelujah psalm." Psalms 41, 72, 89, 106, and 150 each are built around the phrase "Praise the LORD," or, in the original Hebrew, "Hallelujah."*

---

*The Hebrew word *hallelujah* contains the original words *hallel* (praise), *u* (the), *YAH* (short for Yahweh, the original name of God, I AM.) Thus, "praise the Lord."

The hallelujah psalms (and there are more than just these five) are short, powerful songs of praise. These psalms show us that prayer and praise are inseparable, and we're meant to move seamlessly between the two. That each of the five psalm books end with a hallelujah psalm shouts that all our prayers ought finally to end up in praise. After all our lamenting, seeking, confessing, and interceding, we will simply be led to praise the Lord.

What's most beautiful, though, is that Book Five of the Psalter doesn't just end with a single hallelujah psalm. It ends with *five* hallelujah psalms. Psalms 146, 147, 148, and 149 are all simple, powerful songs of praise, and then Psalm 150 is the hallelujah psalm to end all hallelujah psalms.

> Praise the Lord.
>
> Praise God in his sanctuary;
>   praise him in his mighty heavens.
> Praise him for his acts of power;
>   praise him for his surpassing greatness.
> Praise him with the sounding of the trumpet,
>   praise him with the harp and lyre,
> praise him with timbrel and dancing,
>   praise him with the strings and pipe,
> praise him with the clash of cymbals.
>   praise him with resounding cymbals.
>
> Let everything that has breath praise the Lord.
>
> Praise the Lord. (Ps. 150:1–6)

How else would you bring to an end a book of 150 beautiful prayer-songs? "Praise the Lord." Nothing else will do. No other phrase could adequately express the heart of prayer in the end. "Let everything that has breath praise the Lord. Praise the Lord."

In *Answering God*, Eugene Peterson writes this:

> The five Hallelujah Psalms are a cathedral built entirely of praise. No matter how much we suffer, no matter our doubts, no matter how angry we get, no matter how many times we have asked in desperation or doubt, "How long?," prayer develops finally into praise. Everything finds its way to the doorstep of praise. . . . Prayer is always reaching toward praise and will finally arrive there. If we persist in prayer: laugh and cry, doubt and believe, struggle and dance and then struggle again, we will surely end up at Psalm 150, on our feet, applauding, Amen! Amen![14]

Psalm 150 begins and ends with a hallelujah, a "Praise the Lord." First, God's people call to mind what's true about God, that he is worthy of all praise, and it affects them deeply. Israel has been in the wilderness and in the Promised Land; they've been in exile and in Jerusalem; they've dwelled in tents and in the temple. It's not easy being God's people. In everything, they (and we) belong to God. Thus, through Psalm 150, we praise him for who he is ("his acts of power" and "his surpassing greatness"), for where he dwells ("in his sanctuary" and "in the mighty heavens"), and with all we've got ("with the sounding of the trumpet" and "with dancing").

The architecture of the Psalter leads us inevitably to praise. Overall, the dominant lyric of the Psalms shifts from lament in the first half to praise in the second half. The first psalm is about the law; the last psalm is all about praise.

In the end, all prayer turns to praise. All our prayers will get there eventually. We'll be able to make some sense of the ones that were never answered how we hoped. And we'll see that the point of the whole thing was to enjoy time with God and be moved to praise his wonderful name.

Celebration is the overflow of the heart tuned to God. Thanksgiving is continually expressed by those who know how much they have in God, even if they have nothing else. Life will be demanding, and frequently, lament will be our only song. But in the end, it *will* turn to praise. The final word is simply *hallelujah*.

Father,
I praise you for being the Maker of heaven and earth
and Father of kindness and love.
Thank you for this life you have given me.
You are the giver of every good gift,
and I rejoice and give thanks in Christ.
What a joy it is to be your child!
And what a bright, glorious future we have ahead.
Praise you, Father, Son, and Holy Spirit.
Thank you, thank you, thank you.
Hallelujah! Amen.

A Final Word

When my boys were young, I used to take them to Chick-fil-A on my day off. I remember several occasions when, after eating, our youngest son would follow his older brother into the indoor playground. Our tiny youngest son, maybe one or two years old, would quickly climb up to the top. But when he reached the top and looked out from the netting, he would realize how high he was. He'd panic and scream. There was nothing big brother could do to get him down. So, I'd have to fold up my six-foot-three frame and climb up there. Then, with an inconsolable toddler in my arms, I'd have to wiggle and scoot and unfold us both out of there.

Perhaps it's an odd illustration, but prayer is like that. You have to make yourself small to get in, and you have to stay small within it.

There are no experts in prayer. There are only humble children. Our primary goal in starting a praying life is not discipline. It's dependence. The kingdom, after all, belongs not to prophets, priests, and sages but to little children. Prayer—true, real, pour-your-heart-out prayer—often remains hidden from the wise and learned. Only to the young and young-at-heart is it revealed. In prayer, we have to start small.

Once we have begun our praying life, and as we learn a few prayer forms and see some prayers answered, how do we proceed? As the late John Wimber used to say, "The way in is the way on."[1] We don't enter the kingdom of prayer by humility and lowliness and then later graduate into expertise and impressiveness. We don't come into faith by the Spirit then continue by the flesh (Gal. 3:3). We begin as prayer infants and continue as prayer infants. The only prayer "experts" in the New Testament are the Pharisees, and we know how Jesus felt about them. To grow in prayer, we have to remain small.

Praying our hearts out is both the means and the end. It's the way we begin to experience God's presence and power. And it's the goal of life—to live in such intimacy with God that prayer is the ongoing state of our hearts. Or, said another way, the presence of God is both the means and the end. Prayer is merely a continual accessing of God's presence; it's a two-way conversation between Father and child. The presence of God is how we grow, become like Christ, and progress in the Christian life. The presence of God is also the end of our lives; when all our groaning is over, when every tear is wiped away, when all things are made new and there's no need for sun and moon, we will fully enter the presence of God. This is life in the new creation: the presence of God, with no veil and no curtain, no sacrifice and no fasting, no sin and no pain. Oh, my goodness, it will be good.

In the meantime, life with God is a wonderful, painful, beautiful existence. If the way in is the way on, then how do we build a life of childlike, dependent, pour-out-your-heart prayer? A few brief words will be enough, since prayer, at its root, is overflow and not technique. It's not a program to master or a strategy to adopt. It's the glad expression of relationship with our Father. Nonetheless, some practical words may prevent some of the stuck-ness I've experienced in prayer.

Building a Life of Prayer

Developing a prayer routine is more like building a life than anything else. It happens one moment at a time, and we never fully arrive. We rarely notice any growth in ourselves, but over long periods of time, or seen through the eyes of others, transformation and maturity will soon become evident. Consider five small commitments for building a life of prayer.

Make room for prayer.

Although prayer is eventually overflow, it does take much intentionality and practice. It's true of any relationship, of course. When I want to experience greater intimacy with Jessie, I set aside more time. I carefully consider how we might improve our communication, which (like prayer) mostly involves me being more attentive. To connect more deeply with her, or to reconnect with a good friend or family member, I'll need to make time and space for connection and unhurried conversation.

I have found that beginning my day with prayer is essential. I wake up sixty minutes before anyone else in my house, usually between 4:30 and 5:15 a.m., and have coffee ready to brew. There's an old saying, "Going to church on Sunday morning is a Saturday night decision." Getting up for prayer is the same. The evening before, I prepare the coffee, clean up the area in the living room where I pray, and set out my Bible, prayer journal, and 0.38 pen. When I wake, I'm on the couch with coffee and tools in hand within around four minutes. My morning routine includes reading one to three chapters of Scripture, at least one psalm, and writing out my prayers for about 45–60 minutes.

I've also found that one or two more times of prayer throughout the day are immensely helpful to keep the connection strong. Usually by mid-morning or after lunch, I'm feeling frustrated, tired, and disoriented. I typically set aside another mid-day prayer time of 20–30 minutes, and then again before bed, another five to ten minutes. And this doesn't include praying with others, which we'll get to in a moment.

Commit to radical honesty.

We are children of God, and we are fully known and loved. We don't have to hide anything; we don't have to minimize our sin or hide our brokenness. He knows where we are, even when we don't. Bring your real self into his presence, not a cleaned-up, no-mess, curated-social-media version of yourself. He knows you, and he still longs to embrace you.

Embrace your reality.

My old spiritual director, time and time again, would tell me, "Jeremy, you cannot mature in this spiritual life until you embrace your reality." He meant: You might be a college student or a parent of small children or an empty nester with grandchildren, and that's exactly where God has you, so embrace it. You're not living and praying through someone else's life or someone else's season. You're living and praying through *your* reality.

Prayer will look different in different seasons of life. Before we had kids (and I was in seminary with a flexible schedule), I often spent the first three hours of each day in Scripture reading, prayer, and study. But when we had three kids under six and I was pastoring in a large church, just getting ten minutes for prayer was an accomplishment. I had no quiet space in our tiny house, and the moment I set foot out of bed onto our creaky, one-hundred-year-old wood floors, children would awake screaming. Now, with school-aged kids and a growing church to serve and lead, I have found my best prayer rhythms include time praying in solitude, worshipping and praying aloud while driving, and praying with Jessie, my friends, and in prayer meetings.

Further, my prayer life has looked different in seasons when I'm healthy, energetic, and sleeping well than when I am sick, struggling with depression, or suffering from chronic pain and fatigue. You'll likely find yourself praying through seasons of blessing and seasons of heartache, celebration and lament, lightness and despair. It's okay for your prayer life to ebb and flow along with those seasons.

Pray with others.

We've covered this already, but it's too important not to emphasize again. In 2020, after my own season of personal renewal in prayer, our church leadership team reoriented our congregation's rhythms and ministries around prayer. We now have at least two to three prayer meetings weekly, and each of our community groups have an evening of prayer as well. We commit to twenty-four hours of continuous prayer every few months, with additional gatherings throughout those days. Even if your church doesn't offer these gatherings, you can gather a few like-minded friends and set two or three weekly prayer times together. For those of us who regularly pray with others, no one has ever said it's had only a marginal difference in their lives. All of us would say few things have changed our lives more than praying together these last few years.

Establish your rhythms.

Whether alone or with others, praying through different forms and practices will form a house in which your prayers can grow and flourish. Throughout this book, we've considered nine prayer practices. Some of them are true forms of prayer, others help us take a proper posture in prayer (surrender), and still others are prayer-adjacent disciplines (fasting). On the next page is a brief summary of the practices; you can consider them nine ways to pour out your heart.

Perhaps you will recognize one practice that comes naturally—this is a gift to cultivate; seek to build upon this strength and make this practice the core of your prayer life. But you might also find one area most difficult. There is another invitation here: You can continue to grow closer to God and discover increased intimacy with him as you seek to become proficient in this unfamiliar prayer form. There are many more prayer practices too—some that I am just beginning to practice and didn't include in this book. No doubt you are stronger than I in many areas.

Make room for prayer, commit to radical honesty, embrace your reality, pray with others, and establish your rhythms. It will take an eternity to fully learn prayer, and even then, we'll still gladly be novices in the practice of prayer. But that's the point: God is drawing us deeper and deeper into his love.

Nine Ways to Pour Out Your Heart

Practice #1: Reorienting to God (Adoration)

Praising God for his character and goodness, reorienting our hearts and minds to him

Practice #2: Descending with the Mind into the Heart (Contemplation)

Reflecting in a full silence on the goodness of God and our need of him

Practice #3: Collapsing into Jesus (Confession)

Seeking the Father's forgiveness through Jesus for the sin in our lives

Practice #4: On Earth as in Heaven (Intercession)

Praying for others and the expanse of God's kingdom here and now, asking God to be who he is in a specific way

Practice #5: The Most Basic and Important of Prayers (Petition)

Asking the Father for what we want and need

Practice #6: Praying through Heartache (Lament)

Expressing sorrow for the brokenness of the world and seeking God's help

Practice #7: Cultivating a Hunger for God (Fasting)

Refocusing on the Father and his kingdom through short-term self-denial

Practice #8: Giving Up Control of Your Life (Surrender)

Releasing our need for control, receiving God's love, and keeping in step with the Spirit

Practice #9: The Path to Joy and Celebration (Thanksgiving)

Expressing praise and gratitude to the Father for his presence and provision

Returning (Again) to the Father's Love

Where else would we conclude? The Father's love is the spring of living water—which cannot be stopped up or covered—from which all else flows. It's the whole point of prayer. We don't pray simply to get good at prayer, nor do we pray to prove to God we're worthy of his favor. We pray to drop the love of God down deep in our hearts like an anchor. Most deeply, prayer is just the vehicle to experiencing the Father's love.

One day, in the midst of the most significant, exhausting, and heartbreaking situation I've ever experienced, I came home for lunch. Jessie was working from home, and on her lunch break, she was reading and praying. As I collapsed into a kitchen chair, she excitedly told me about what she was reading. She began to read from Isaiah 43.

> Now this is what the LORD says—
> > the one who created you, Jacob,
> > the one who formed you, Israel—
> "Do not fear, for I have redeemed you;
> > I have called you by name; you are mine.
> When you pass through the waters,
> > I will be with you, and the rivers will not overwhelm you.
> When you walk through the fire,
> > you will not be scorched, and the flame will not burn you.
> For I am the LORD your God,
> > the Holy One of Israel, and your Savior."
> (Isa. 43:1–3 CSB)

As she read, tears began to fill my eyes. I'm not frequently a crier. But this day, I couldn't hold it in. Tears poured down my face. Jessie was startled; she had never seen anything like it from me. Giant, heavy sobs shook my body.

> "Because you are precious in my sight
> and honored, and I love you,
> I will give people in exchange for you
> and nations instead of your life.
> Do not fear, for I am with you."
> (Isa. 43:4–5 CSB)

This is perhaps the clearest, most compelling passage on God's love for you in all the Bible. God is leaning toward us, even now, calling out: Pay attention! This morning, this evening, wherever you are sitting or standing. He calls out to you and me: *My child, hear my heart and believe. I am the Lord your God. I have given much in exchange for you. You have no idea how much it cost me. But because you are precious to me, because I love you with a never-ending love—my child, I am with you!*

All we have to do is receive. Receive the embrace of the Father who waits for us.

How many of us are still living like orphans—unsure of our place, not secure in anyone's love, we fight and defend our way through life? Or, how many of us are still living like mere servants—we are willing to serve our master, we want to please him, and we're working hard around his house?

How often we live like the orphan or the servant, even though we've been adopted, we've been welcomed inside. The family robe is on our shoulders, the feast has been prepared for us. Why would we remain outside doing work, when our Father stands at the door and says, "Come, my child; come and eat with me!"

Remember this truth we explored some pages back: Our God has everything he needs. He doesn't need more servants; he doesn't need an army of obedient soldiers. He needs nothing. But he wants something. He wants children who delight in him, as he delights in them. Can you believe it?

Receiving the love of the Father is your life's most important work.

Yeah, I said it. Your life's most important work is not your spiritual disciplines, your marriage or parenting, your ministry, your job, and it's definitely not building up savings or accumulating impressive objects.

Your life's most important work is learning how to receive and live in the love of your heavenly Father. Your most important work is a non-work. And it's what every one of us needs more than anything. It's what the church needs in a state of decline, and it's what our neighbors and coworkers and family members need more than anything.

The love of God is the most important thing in all the world. It's the treasure, hidden in a field. Sell everything you have and get this one thing, because having it, you'll have riches beyond your dreams. It's the coin that the old woman lost, so she swept out her whole house till she found it, because it's more valuable than life itself.

The love of God will make you radically secure, and he wants to pour it into your heart. Will you receive it?

"Our Father in heaven,
    hallowed be your name;

your kingdom come,
your will be done,
>	on earth as it is in heaven.
Give us today our daily bread.
And forgive us our debts,
>	as we also have forgiven our debtors.
And lead us not into temptation,
>	but deliver us from the evil one."

(Matt. 6:9–13)

For yours is the kingdom and the power and the glory, forever and ever.

Hallelujah! Hallelujah! Amen and amen.

Acknowledgments

I have always been a fan of 90s and 2000s hip-hop—the smooth, old-school stuff, not the trendy, wildly explicit new stuff. And many of my favorite rap albums have "ride-out tracks," a closing song that's not really a song. Set to a simple beat, it's a rapper's rambling list of gratitude. (And, sure, sometimes haters are identified and blasted.) Done well, it's one of the great contributions of hip-hop to our universe.

Anyway, I think of book acknowledgments as an author's ride-out track. Feel free to put on an instrumental beat in the background as you read. This is my first full-length book, so I'm going to enjoy this. If you're not into the credits, no need to stay in the theater.

To my wonderful wife, Jessie, thank you. I am so in love with you, so thankful for your friendship, and so much more like Christ because of you. Thank you for providing non-stop support for my pastoral life, and thank you for all the time spent praying together. Thank you for providing so much direct encouragement to write and keep on writing—and for reading and making suggestions on every chapter. This book would not exist without your love and support. I love you!

Shout-out to our three wild boys—Joseph, Jude, and Jack. You guys are awesome. I worked on this book only during work hours, before sunrise, and while you were at school . . . because I didn't want to give up a minute with you guys! I love who God is making each of you, and I can't wait to see you grow up in Christ. And now, this book is done, so get your sneaks and let's play some ball.

Thank you to the pastors, leaders, and members of Trinity Community Church. You all are my joy and delight. It is an absolute honor to serve as one of your pastors, and I hope you'll keep me around for a while. Thank you to our pastors for carrying additional shepherding and teaching burdens to provide me with time to read, reflect, and write. Thank you to our elders and staff over the last six years—Mark, Casey, Joe, Cam, Lauren, Becca, Kate, Madison, Allison, Austin, Dan, Helena, and Will. Thank you to our members for your constant encouragement, prayer, and support. Thank you for letting me work out so much of the heart and content of this book over the last four years.

Shout-out to our dearest friends, especially Mark and Allison, Cam and Kayla. Love you guys! Shout-out to Tyler and Sarah, my Ball Don't Lie group, and my Fellowship Associates guys. My good friend Ben passed away suddenly while I was working on this book. Man, we miss you. Julie, we love you and we're with you!

Shout-out to the many pastors, leaders, and spiritual directors who have generously poured their time and energy into me as a young pastor—Kevin Larson, Daniel Montgomery, Kevin Jamison, Rich Plass, Eric Johnson, Bill Wellons, Jay Fowler, Scotty Smith, Sam Storms, and countless others. Shout-out to Harbor Network; thanks for walking with us through some stuff. Shout-out to Collin Hansen, Ivan Mesa, and everyone at The Gospel Coalition for ten years of writing opportunities.

Thank you to the many authors who have written books or preached on prayer that have changed me deeply: J. I. Packer, Tim Keller, and Eugene Peterson most of all. Thank you also to Henri Nouwen, Richard Lovelace, John Wimber, Terry Virgo, John Piper, Jack Miller, Jon Tyson, and so many more. Shout-out to Wendell Berry also. My guy.

Thank you to my parents, Terry and Dawn, who raised me in a Spirit-filled church and taught me how to pray. Thank you for everything. Thank you to Chuck and Jenny for raising the best woman ever; thank you for all your support as well. Thank you to our whole network of extended family members and supportive friends. It's so good to be home. My friend Sammy: thank you for all the conversations and prayers over almost four decades.

My brother, Joe, died when I was sixteen. I miss you, man. Hope to see you soon. My little sis, Sarah, I love you!

Thank you to Uprise Bakery, for letting me write in your space every Tuesday and Friday morning for six years. Sorry I've still never spent more than $2.98. Thanks to the Avett Brothers, Kanye West, J Cole, Lecrae, and Mav City for providing the soundtrack while working on this book.

Thank you to my book team—my agent, Don Gates, my editor, Ashley Gorman, and to the whole team at B&H. Thanks for taking a chance on a nobody pastor in a nobody place. Thanks for believing in this project. Y'all are great. Let's do this thing again some time.

I won't say anything about the publishers that passed on this book. I'll save that for some other ride-out track. I'm sure you're all wonderful folks and wish you the best.

Thank you, dear reader, for making it this far (or like I do, for opening the book straight to the acknowledgments to figure out if this author is worth reading). I hope and pray this little book has been a blessing to you. I've been praying for you all along. Let me know when you're coming through central Missouri, and we'll put a coffee and prayer meeting on the calendar.

Shout-out to the pastors, church planters, and missionaries all over the world. Women and men following Jesus, striving in prayer, extending the kingdom of God: I praise and thank God for you. I had you in mind while writing.

Father God, my goodness. Thank you, thank you, thank you. Thank you for this life; thank you for putting a heart for prayer in me. Thank you, Lord Jesus, for your life, your death, your resurrection. Thank you for appearing to me in that awful hospital the night Joe died. (That's a story for another book.) Holy Spirit of God, thank you for opening my eyes to you more and more these past four years especially. At times, I felt like your words were flowing through me into sentences and paragraphs. Increase in me and in this place, Spirit of God!

Alright, friends, thanks for bearing with me. Please forgive me for anything in this book that proves unhelpful, or if I've missed giving credit to anyone for a thought or theme. If you've found anything helpful, praise the Lord.

Notes

Introduction
1. Ricky Gervais, Netflix special, *"Supernature,"* 2022.

Chapter 1
1. Ray Ortlund on *You're Not Crazy: Gospel Sanity for Young Pastors* podcast, season 1, episode 1.
2. Sally Lloyd-Jones, *The Jesus Storybook Bible: Every Story Whispers His Name* (Grand Rapids: Zondervan, 2007), 222.
3. Lloyd-Jones, *The Jesus Storybook Bible*, 169.
4. J. I. Packer, *Knowing God* (Downers Grove, IL: InterVarsity, 1993), 201.
5. Richard F. Lovelace, *Dynamics of Spiritual Life: An Evangelical Theology of Renewal* (1979: repr., Downers Grove, IL: InterVarsity, 2020), 212.
6. Jon Tyson sermon series "Converting the Church," in October 2022; John Starke, *The Secret Place of Thunder: Trading Our Need to Be Noticed for a Hidden Life with Christ* (Grand Rapids, Zondervan, 2023), 15–31.
7. Jon Tyson sermon series "Converting the Church."

Chapter 3
1. Henri J. M. Nouwen, *Life of the Beloved: Spiritual Living in a Secular World* (Chestnut Ridge, NY: Crossroad Publishing, 1992), 59.
2. John Stott, *The Cross of Christ* (Downers Grove, IL: InterVarsity, 1986), 335.
3. Charles Spurgeon, *The Treasury of David*, Volume 2 (1869; repr., Nashville: Thomas Nelson, 1996), 51.

Chapter 4

1. Michael Easter, "Leverage the Power of Silence," Two Percent newsletter, December 15, 2022, https://www.twopct.com/p/leverage-the-power-of-silence?utm_source=publication-search.
2. Easter, "Leverage the Power of Silence."
3. Tim Keller, "Studies in Prayer" (2007) small group study, available at gospelinlife.com.
4. Henri J. M. Nouwen, *The Way of the Heart: Desert Spirituality and Contemporary Ministry* (New York: Harper & Row, 1981), 9.
5. Nouwen, *The Way of the Heart*, 10–11.
6. Nouwen, *The Way of the Heart*, 15.
7. Tyler Staton, *Praying like Monks, Living like Fools: An Invitation to the Wonder and Mystery of Prayer* (Grand Rapids: Zondervan, 2022), 14.
8. J. I. Packer, *Praying the Lord's Prayer* (Wheaton, IL: Crossway, 2007), 11.
9. Packer, *Praying the Lord's Prayer*, 57.
10. Packer, *Praying the Lord's Prayer*, 41.
11. Raymond C. Ortlund Jr., *Isaiah: God Saves Sinners* (Wheaton, IL: Crossway, 2005), 75.
12. Tim Keller, "Isaiah and the Altar" sermon, November 24, 1996, Redeemer Presbyterian Church.
13. Donald S. Whitney, *Praying the Bible* (Wheaton, IL: Crossway, 2015), 48–51.
14. Martin Laird, *Into the Silent Land: A Guide to the Christian Practice of Contemplation* (New York: Oxford University Press, 2006), 1–2.
15. Dane Ortlund, *Gentle and Lowly: The Heart of Christ for Sinners and Sufferers* (Wheaton, IL: Crossway, 2020). Dane makes this point wonderfully and finds, in my opinion, the right balance of demonstrating Jesus's patient heart for us sinners without giving an ounce of license to sin.
16. George Mueller, quoted in John Piper, *The Marks of a Spiritual Leader*, PDF version, 12–13, https://document.desiringgod.org/the-marks-of-a-spiritual-leader-en.pdf?ts=1446648296.
17. Richard J. Foster, *Celebration of Discipline: The Path to Spiritual Growth* (New York: HarperCollins, 1998), 1.

Chapter 5

1. See my article "The Lord's Prayer Is Meant to Be Lived," The Gospel Coalition, August 6, 2022, https://www.thegospelcoalition.org/article/lords-prayer-lived/.
2. N. T. Wright, *The Lord and His Prayer* (Grand Rapids: Eerdmans, 1996), 9.

3. Frederick Buechner, *Whistling in the Dark: A Doubter's Dictionary* (New York: HarperCollins, 1988), 84.

4. See Charles Spurgeon, *Only a Prayer Meeting: Studies on Prayer Meetings and Prayer Meeting Addresses*, revised (Fearn, Ross-shire: Christian Focus Publications, 2010).

5. C. John Miller, *Powerful Evangelism for the Powerless* (Phillipsburg, NJ: P&R Publishing, 1997), 63.

Chapter 6

1. J. I. Packer, *Knowing God* (Downers Grove, IL: InterVarsity, 1993), 243.
2. Packer, *Knowing God*, 245.
3. Chuck Palahniuk, *Fight Club: A Novel* (New York: W. W. Norton & Co., 1996), 166.
4. Dietrich Bonhoeffer, *Life Together* (New York: Harper & Row, 1954), 26.
5. Bonhoeffer, *Life Together*, 26.
6. Packer, *Knowing God*, 246.
7. Tim Keller, *Walking with God through Pain and Suffering* (New York: Penguin Group, 2013), 5–6.
8. Keller, *Walking with God through Pain and Suffering*, 6.
9. Packer, *Knowing God*, 250, emphasis added.
10. Richard Plass, in a personal conversation.
11. Mark Sayers, *A Non-Anxious Presence* (Chicago: Moody, 2022), 107.
12. Sayers, *A Non-Anxious Presence*, 107.
13. I am indebted to Tim Keller for this illustration from one of his sermons.
14. J. I. Packer and Carolyn Nystrom, *Praying: Finding Our Way through Duty into Delight* (Downers Grove, IL: InterVarsity, 2006), 215.
15. Timothy Keller, *Prayer* (New York: Penguin Books, 2016), 228.
16. Sally Lloyd-Jones, *The Jesus Storybook Bible: Every Story Whispers His Name* (Grand Rapids: Zondervan, 2007), 304.
17. For more on the theme of Jesus's presence in our pain, see Stephen Seamands' *Follow the Healer: Biblical and Theological Foundations for Healing Ministry* (Grand Rapids: Zondervan, 2023), 112–30.

Chapter 7

1. Peter Brown, *Augustine of Hippo: A Biography* (Berkeley: University of California Press, 1967), 375.
2. John Piper, *A Hunger for God: Desiring God through Fasting and Prayer* (Wheaton, IL: Crossway, 1997), 23.

3. Eugene H. Peterson, *Leap Over a Wall: Earthy Spirituality for Everyday Christians* (New York: HarperCollins, 1998), 152.

4. Charles Spurgeon, *Treasury of David*, abridged by David O. Fuller (Grand Rapids: Kregel, 1968), Psalm 27:4, p. 136, emphasis added.

5. Søren Kierkegaard, *Purity of Heart Is to Will One Thing: Spiritual Preparation for the Office of Confession* (1938; repr., New York: Harper & Row, 1956).

6. Tim Keller, "Isaiah and the Altar" sermon, November 24, 1996.

7. Sally Lloyd-Jones, *The Jesus Storybook Bible: Every Story Whispers His Name* (Grand Rapids: Zondervan, 2007), 314.

8. I'm deeply grateful to Ashley Gorman for her reflections on the John 20 encounter.

9. Edward Farrell, *Prayer Is a Hunger*, quoted in John Piper, *A Hunger for God*, 12.

10. Piper, *A Hunger for God*, 23.

11. Mark Sayers, *The Portland Sessions* podcast, Part 5.

12. Richard J. Foster, *Celebration of Discipline: The Path to Spiritual Growth* (New York: HarperCollins, 1998), 55.

13. Wendell Berry, "I Dream of a Quiet Man" poem in *Given* (Berkeley, CA: Counterpoint, 2005), 70.

Chapter 8

1. Michael Green, *Thirty Years That Changed the World: The Book of Acts for Today* (Grand Rapids: Eerdmans, 2002), 7–8.

2. Green, *Thirty Years That Changed the World*, 8.

3. Green, *Thirty Years That Changed the World*, 268.

4. Green, *Thirty Years That Changed the World*, 271.

5. Ray Ortlund on *You're Not Crazy: Gospel Sanity for Young Pastors* podcast, season 1, episode 1.

6. I'm grateful to my friend Kevin Cawley for this illustration.

7. Francis Schaeffer, *The Lord's Work in the Lord's Way and No Little People* (1974; repr., Wheaton, IL: Crossway, 2022), 32, emphasis added.

8. See the Prayer of Saint Augustine, quoted in Gregg Allison, *God, Gift, and Guide: Knowing the Holy Spirit* (Brentwood, TN: B&H Publishing Group, 2023), ix.

9. Schaeffer, *The Lord's Work*, 36.

10. Schaeffer, *The Lord's Work*, 52.

11. C. John Miller, *The Heart of a Servant Leader: Letters from Jack Miller* (Phillipsburg, NJ: P&R Publishing, 2004), 90–92.

Chapter 9

1. UCLA Health, "Health Benefits of Gratitude," March 22, 2023, https://www.uclahealth.org/news/health-benefits-gratitude.

2. E. T. Bohlmeijer, J. T. Kraiss, P. Watkins et al., "Promoting Gratitude as a Resource for Sustainable Mental Health: Results of a 3-Armed Randomized Controlled Trial up to 6 Months Follow-up," *Journal of Happiness Studies* 22 (2021):1011–32, https://doi.org/10.1007/s10902-020-00261-5.

3. Lilian Jans-Beken, Nele Jacobs, Mayke Janssens, Sanne Peeters, Jennifer Reijnders, Lilian Lechner, and Johan Lataster (2019): "Gratitude and health: An updated review," *The Journal of Positive Psychology* (August 2019), DOI: 10.1080/17439760.2019.1651888.

4. Meister Eckhart as quoted in Susyn Reeve, *The Wholehearted Life: Big Changes and Greater Happiness Week by Week* (Berkeley, CA: Cleis Press, 2014), 69.

5. Ronald Rolheiser, *Sacred Fire: A Vision for a Deeper Human and Christian Maturity* (New York: Penguin, 2014), 244.

6. Rolheiser, *Sacred Fire*, 245.

7. Andrew Wilson, *Spirit and Sacrament: An Invitation to Eucharismatic Worship* (Grand Rapids: Zondervan, 2018), 29.

8. E. M. Bounds, *E. M. Bounds on Prayer* (New Kensington, PA: Whitaker House, 1997), 307.

9. Bounds, *E. M. Bounds on Prayer*, 308.

10. C. S. Lewis, *The Weight of Glory* (New York: HarperOne, 2006), 34.

11. Dallas Willard, *Life without Lack: Living in the Fullness of Psalm 23* (Nashville: Thomas Nelson, 2018), ix.

12. Wendell Berry, *Hannah Coulter: A Novel* (Berkeley, CA: Counterpoint, 2004), 113.

13. John Starke, *The Possibility of Prayer: Finding Stillness with God in a Restless World* (Downers Grove, IL: InterVarsity, 2020), 9.

14. Eugene Peterson, *Answering God: The Psalms as Tools for Prayer* (New York: HarperCollins, 1991), 127.

Final Word

1. For this quote and other "Wimberisms," see Glenn Schroder, *Never Trust a Leader without a Limp: The Wit and Wisdom of John Wimber, Founder of the Vineyard Church Movement* (Nashville: Thomas Nelson, 2020).

More Books to Help You Grow in Your Prayer Life

Available Wherever Books Are Sold